Communicate
to win

2ND EDITION

Communicate
to win

RICHARD DENNY

Lon

Throughout the book 'he' and 'she' are used liberally. If there is a preponderance of the masculine pronoun it is because the inadequacies of the English language do not provide a single personal pronoun suitable to refer to both sexes.

Publisher's note
Every possible effort has been made to ensure that the information contained in this book is accurate at the time of going to press, and the publishers and authors cannot accept responsibility for any errors or omissions, however caused. No responsibility for loss or damage occasioned to any person acting, or refraining from action, as a result of the material in this publication can be accepted by the editor, the publisher or any of the authors.

First published in Great Britain by Kogan Page in 2001
Second edition published in 2006

120 Pentonville Road
London N1 9JN
United Kingdom
www.kogan-page.co.uk

525 South 4th Street, #241
Philadelphia, PA 19147
USA

British Library Cataloguing in Publication Data

A CIP record for this book is available from the British Library.

ISBN 0 7494 4435 5

Typeset by Jean Cussons Typesetting, Diss, Norfolk
Printed and bound in the United States by Thomson-Shore, Inc

123853

Thank you to Judith Harker for her loyalty and
commitment through turbulent
times – you are really appreciated

Contents

Introduction

'Communication' is one of the most important words in the English language. Without communication, businesses would founder, governments fall. Yet lack of communication, and the inability of people to communicate effectively, cause a large amount of stress, frustration, anger, resentment, misunderstanding and disappointment. How often have we heard and used such phrases as 'If only you'd told me', 'Why didn't you say so?', 'You didn't make yourself clear' and so on?

Good communication skills are absolutely vital in any successful workplace. The ability to impart information and instructions clearly and concisely and so that they are easily understood can determine whether or not you get your message across to a customer or colleague, or clinch that deal. Whether you are dealing with the secretary in the next office, the workforce on the shop floor or the salesman out on the road, your skill in telling people what they need to know is the key to them performing at their best. Conversely, their ability to give feedback to management can have a huge influence on the continued success and prosperity of the company.

So, what is this book about, who is it for, and what will readers get out of it? It is a snapshot of the vast subject of communication, and in particular interpersonal communication and the various methods of communication – the spoken and the written word, the one-to-one conversation and the gathering around the conference table. In short, Part 1 is about any situation where two or more people get together (or exchange written messages) to discuss company policy, thrash out problems, plan courses of action, take positive decisions. Part 2 is dedicated to presentation skills.

Those reading this book will be committed to self-improvement and self-help. They will aspire to greater success and through that success greater enjoyment, confidence and happiness in their professional life. They will want to progress from the 'I wish I could' syndrome and join the 'I can' and 'I will' clubs. They will seek to improve the quality of their life through self-fulfilment and greater achievement in the workplace.

By following the principles and taking note of the practical examples set out in this book readers will be able to improve their communication skills and achieve a level of communication they never imagined they were capable of attaining. Those who felt that their inability to communicate adequately was holding them back will find themselves unshackled; those who perhaps thought they were good communicators already will be amazed to discover hidden reserves. Whatever your profession and your goals in life, the better you can communicate, the more you will achieve.

Part 1

Communication Skills

The Importance of Communication

More change has taken place in the past 30 years than in the whole history of humankind. This change has included ever-increasing technological advances to enable us to communicate faster, more efficiently and more effectively.

Technological changes have indisputably led to faster and more efficient communication. We have e-mail, text messaging with its abbreviated language (in fact a whole new language), fax machines, telephones, telephone conferencing, video conferencing and pagers, but are we communicating more effectively? No.

We have TV and radio stations that transmit news immediately, newspapers, journals, trade magazines, newsletters, books, direct mail, specialist publications and the world wide web. We are getting to the point of information overload, but are we communicating more effectively? No.

Children today have less opportunity to communicate and learn people skills than ever before. Many rush out to school having eaten breakfast on their own. In the classroom they are under pressure to achieve academically. There is less time to play and interact with other pupils than in the past, less participation in sport and even less time for human relationship skills. Back at home, many children eat a meal in front of the

TV, again often on their own, then probably do their homework and spend a few hours in front of the computer. Television is not conducive to conversation. Of course it has great value; but when it's on you can be sure that conversation will dwindle. As a result, people have become increasingly introverted, less willing to share feelings and emotions, and have little time or inclination to converse with friends and family.

In many homes it is rare for a family to sit round a table and eat a meal together. Family activities like these can be quality time, and it's amazing how, during these times, we can resolve worries, problems, upsets and misunderstandings. Yet this very rarely happens, to the detriment of many relationships.

Marriage break-ups, divorce and domestic strife all seem to be on the increase. Of course there are many reasons – pressures of work, pressures of debt and so on – but the family environment used to be the greatest vaccination against human conflict. In this environment children were guided and unacceptable behaviour was corrected. There were role models that not only created security, but by example demonstrated good practice. Also, people knew their neighbours and had time to talk. There was always someone to talk to. Relationships were valued. Sadly, things have changed. Let's state the obvious: firstly, you have got you for the rest of your life; and secondly, your happiness will be enhanced by your ability to communicate more effectively.

The world wide web and e-mail of course have great value and use. The majority of people use the web wisely to gather information which saves vast amounts of time, and there is a massive range of information and sources to choose from that enables us to speak to the right person for the right solution.

Everything that we do throughout each day involves communication in one form or another – at work and at home, in politics, commerce, education, sport, entertainment and the financial world. Communication touches every sphere of our lives. Yet communication is a largely undervalued, untaught asset in the modern world, often with disastrous results. When communication breaks down, the bombs and the brickbats start flying about – whether in the home environment, the workplace or the global political arena. Professor Stephen Hawking of Cambridge University stated in a TV commercial, which in my opinion was the most powerful TV commercial I have ever seen, that 'the world's problems could be solved if we kept talking'. This idea can be applied to almost any situation.

Whether it is two individuals in a small organization or two radical groups in an international conflict, if they don't communicate they will never resolve their differences.

Communication in Education

Education is all about communication – not only of hard facts but also of thoughts and ideas and proposals on which to base discussion and debate. A good teacher who can effectively communicate facts, ideas and theories will turn out well-qualified pupils, but there is one thing lacking in almost every education system in the world, and that is teaching those pupils how to communicate their thoughts to others. Young people are simply not being prepared for what the world needs, or for them to be able to achieve the success and enjoyment that are available.

There is a common belief among educationalists that knowledge is power. This is totally incorrect. Knowledge is not power; it is potential power. We get paid for what we do with what we know, not just for what we know. When we have gained knowledge, what is most important is how we use it – how we communicate it, or pass it on to others.

Consider the following statement: formal education has one purpose only – to get people their first job. Self-education earns them their living.

Initially, the truth of this statement may be difficult to accept.

However, although aspects of what we learn at school, college or university enable us to get through our first interview, how much of what we learn in our years of formal education do we actually use later on in life? If we are honest, very little.

The Business Environment

One of my clients takes on 1,000 university graduates every year. These graduates are intelligent, well qualified, and keen to find a job in today's competitive market. Yet within 12 months 60 per cent of them have left the company. Why? Some are simply not up to it, or find that the work doesn't suit them, but the largest single reason for this alarmingly high drop-out rate is the graduates' inability to communicate with their peers and their superiors.

You can acquire great knowledge, but unless you can communicate to others, it is worthless.

HR directors and personnel managers have said that they have problems finding people who can communicate effectively. This, I suggest, goes back to the education system, where teachers are simply not teaching their students how to communicate, and therefore not preparing them for the business world. There are two really obvious solutions to this dilemma. One is that each teacher should spend at least one week per year working in the commercial environment. And secondly, that every senior or middle management executive should spend at least five days per year in schools sharing their experiences with our young people.

In many cases, problems due to a lack of communication in the workplace can start on day one. Here is a typical example:

A arrives for his first day in a new job. B is delegated to show him the ropes.

What does B do? He has worked here for some time: he knows it all backwards. So he paints only a broad picture, leaving out minor details which are second nature to him but not at all obvious to A.

How does A react? He has an awful lot to digest in his first few days. He is nervous and perhaps a little shy, which does not help his concentration.

What happens next? A begins to realize that he needs more information in order to do the job properly. B, in the meantime, considers he has done his bit, and goes back to his own workload. A is too nervous or embarrassed to ask questions that might be considered stupid.

The result? A is already struggling: he is unable to perform to his best ability. His self-confidence is crumbling. B begins to think that A is not up to the job.

A member of my family, Richard, who is 19, arrived for his first day albeit as a temporary worker in a window frame manufacturing operation. He walked up to his new boss, put out his hand to shake hands and gave his name. The boss simply raised his right hand, pointing across the workshop and said 'over there'. Not only did he not shake hands, he didn't welcome this young man, he did absolutely nothing to make him feel wanted or valued on his first day at work.

This little story indicates not only a total lack of manners, but a gross misunderstanding of the importance of communication. This particular company has massive staff turnover, obviously.

The lesson?

▓ Communicate from the word go.
▓ Explain things clearly and in detail.
▓ Don't think that because something is obvious to you, it must be obvious to someone else.

■ If you are the one being trained, don't be afraid to say things like 'I get the overall picture, but would you please go through such-and-such a point again?'
■ Ask questions.
■ Talk.

For management the cost of failed communication can be absolutely staggering, involving:

■ loss of time;
■ loss of respect;
■ loss of business;
■ loss of money;
■ loss of confidence;
■ loss of credibility;
■ loss of relationships;
■ loss of staff;
■ loss of trust;
■ loss of clients.

But when communication is good, the benefits are immediately apparent. People:

■ feel good;
■ do their job well;
■ work well together;
■ feel motivated;
■ understand;
■ save time;
■ feel empowered;
■ assume responsibility;
■ share information;
■ respect, trust and like each other;
■ listen.

Poor communication will inevitably lead to a negative outcome. Effective communication will undoubtedly lead to a positive one.

In the modern world there is a more urgent need than ever for people at the top to be able to communicate with others. This applies to those holding positions of achievement or power in politics, business, sport, entertainment or any other sphere of life.

It would be impossible for anyone in any public company or position to hold his or her job without mastering the skills of how to communicate with employees, handle the media, or speak in public. However, there must be a balance – it is important to have knowledge but you must also have the ability to communicate that knowledge effectively.

Throughout this book we will be looking at a range of scenarios, situations and styles to enable people to communicate more effectively. If you are going to win with communication you have to be prepared and able to face every situation. In the long run, the more open you are, the more you are prepared to talk and ask questions, the more you are prepared to build relationships, the more you will find that good interpersonal communication will be a great winner for you.

Pocket Reminders

- Create quality talk time with family and friends
- Learn to communicate your knowledge to others
- Talk about misunderstandings: be constructive
- Don't be afraid to ask questions
- Keep talking.

Wise Words

Nobody can go back to start a new beginning, but anyone can start today to make a new ending.

Maria Robinson

2

Interpersonal Communication

It is often said that the ability to communicate well with others is a skill that successful people have mastered. As success cannot really be achieved without input from other people, it follows that good communication skill becomes a vital and necessary ingredient.

> If you want to be more successful, the better you are able to communicate, the more you will achieve.

It is also often said – wrongly – that a good communicator is someone who speaks well.

> Less than 10 per cent of any personal communication that makes an impression is of the verbal kind.

There is obviously much more to communication excellence than just being able to talk well. It takes at least two people to communicate interpersonally, so what do they see, hear and feel during this process? You can be absolutely clear and unambiguous, but the person you are communicating with can give you a totally unexpected reaction, resulting in complete misunderstanding. For example:

Communicator 1: 'I've brought you Polly's telephone number.'

Communicator 2: 'I can't phone her now – I'm too busy.'

Communicator 1: 'I didn't ask you to phone her *now*!'

Here Communicator 1 was absolutely clear, with an unambiguous message apparently unlikely to cause any misunderstanding, but he or she got an unexpectedly hostile reaction from Communicator 2, who completely misinterpreted Communicator 1's good intentions. No wonder we all think 'We are just not communicating' from time to time.

We can psychoanalyse the above example endlessly, but I would simply like to draw your attention to Communicator 2. Have you reacted the way this person did? Communication is not just what we say or do: it is also what we hear and see. If we are going to excel in communication it is necessary to respond to other people, rather than react, and there is a difference. Think of it in terms of a doctor's prescription – if you respond to the medicine it is doing you good, if you react it is not, and you need a change of medicine.

Using All Your Senses

Let's first identify the ways in which people process information. Normally, there are five major senses:

▓ visual;
▓ kinaesthetic (feeling);
▓ auditory (hearing);
▓ taste;
▓ smell.

Most of us are fortunate to possess all five senses, but we will concentrate on the three major communication areas – the visual, kinaesthetic and auditory senses. It is important to accept at this stage that most people use all three. However, people are different in that some will use one area more predominantly than the other two.

So, how do you process information? Is your predominant sense visual, kinaesthetic or auditory? It is important to be aware of this, because to excel as a communicator you not only need to have a greater understanding of other people, but also need to have a greater understanding of yourself. This is known as emotional intelligence (EQ), which we will discuss in more detail later.

Here is a list of phrases that enable you to identify a person's predominant sense.

▓ Visualise cue phrases: 'see the sense'; 'looks to me like'; 'appears to me'; 'short-sighted'; 'see eye to eye'.

Predominantly visual people normally speak fairly quickly, because they think in pictures. They try to make the speed of their words keep up with the speed of the pictures in their mind. They may greet you by saying 'Nice to see you.'

▓ Kinaesthetic cue phrases: 'it feels right'; 'get to grips with'; 'hand in hand'; 'slipped my mind'; 'let's lay the cards on the table'.

Predominantly kinaesthetic types normally speak fairly slowly, because they are reacting to their feelings and some-times have trouble finding the right words to match those feelings. They may greet you by saying 'How are you?', which of course means 'How are you feeling?'.

▓ Auditory cue phrases: 'I hear what you're saying'; 'loud and clear'; 'unheard of'; 'word for word'.

Predominantly auditory people also speak fairly slowly with a well-modulated voice, using words carefully and selectively. They may greet you with 'I heard you were coming today', or they may say 'I hear the job's going well'.

It is easy to see how two people who share the same predominant sense can communicate well with each other, while two people who have different predominant senses can find themselves talking at cross purposes, leading to a communication breakdown and the message not getting through.

If you encounter difficulties communicating with someone with a different predominant sense, what is the answer? Very simple – just change the language in order to communicate more effectively. Use the appropriate language for the appropriate person, both spoken and written. If you are a predominantly kinaesthetic person talking to a predominantly visual type, use expressions such as 'I see it this way', or 'It doesn't look right', rather than 'My feeling is', or 'I don't feel comfortable with this'.

The subconscious effect of this is often called creating communication rapport or, more commonly, creating the right chemistry. Have you ever met someone for the first time and instinctively disliked them? This is commonly referred to as 'bad chemistry' or 'bad vibes', but it is often down to the fact that you are not talking the same language when it comes to communicating. Conversely, two people with the same predominant sense will probably get on very well right from the start.

To modify one's communication style is really quite simple. All you have to do is listen to the type of words and phrases the other person is using consistently. This leads on to one of the golden rules of communication:

Listen and listen well.

Being a great communicator is not just dependent on your ability to talk and write well. It is equally important to be an excellent listener.

How to Listen Well

We learn more by listening than we ever do by talking, so it is absolutely crucial to listen well. It is claimed that a woman can listen to two or three conversations simultaneously, whereas a man can only listen to one at a time.

We have two ears and one mouth and that is the ratio by which they are best used. Here are three important points to bear in mind while listening to someone:

▦ Look the other person in the eye.
▦ Concentrate entirely on what they are saying.
▦ Check that you have not misunderstood a word or a phrase. This will aid the concentration and the listening process.

Use the following test to see whether someone is listening well. Ask a colleague to write down the answers to these questions:

▦ How many of each *species* did Moses take into the Ark?
▦ Some months have 31 days, some have 30 days. How many have 28 days?
▦ Guy Fawkes, bonfire night, gunpowder plot etc. Do they have a 5th of November in the United States?

Now the answers:

▦ How many of each species? Two? No. One? No. Your colleague scores a point for saying it was Noah, not Moses, who went into the Ark.
▦ Who said that only February has 28 days? (All 12 months have 28 days in them.)
▦ Yes, they do have a 5th of November in the United States, and a 6th, a 7th and so on!

These three examples illustrate just how important it is to listen really well. It is vital in any form of communication, and remember too that a good listener is usually more popular than someone who talks a lot.

What does a listener look like?

▨ The listener keeps looking at the speaker (without staring) although the speaker may look away.

▨ The listener's body is open, arms are not folded and the hands are open and in view.

▨ The listener is more likely to be smiling rather than frowning and with a pleasant and encouraging expression.

▨ The listener will often be leaning towards the other person, not away from them.

Be Yourself

Let's imagine the hypothetical situation of two people facing each other across a table. There are two human beings present, but there are six personalities.

On one side is me – the person I think I am, the person I am giving the impression I am, and the real me. On the other side is you – the person you think you are, the person you are giving me the impression you are, and the real you.

At this stage, in order to establish effective communication, it is vital to get the two real people communicating with one another. So, what do you do?

The answer is simple. Firstly, be yourself, not a performer. Secondly, control your imagination – don't lapse into fantasy. Thirdly, ask questions that will identify the real person opposite you, and watch the body language that goes with the answers.

Forgive me for stating the obvious, but a conversation is a two-way process. It's not one person talking – and the other supposedly listening. If you believe you are not a good conversationalist, the easiest and most effective way to improve is as follows:

To begin with you must show interest in the other person with your body language, through eye to eye contact and full frontal body language. Now the easiest way to start a conversation is of course with a question. And remember, here the conversation is not a conversation when one person is speaking and the other person is not listening, but thinking what they are going to say next.

Example A: How to do it

Are you taking a holiday this year?

Yes.

Where are you going?

Tenerife.

Oh how lovely, why did you choose Tenerife?

We went there three years ago and it was fantastic.

Why was it fantastic?

The hotel was exquisite, the views outstanding and the climate was brilliant.

Where were you staying?

Example B: How not to do it

Are you taking a holiday this year?

Yes.

Where are you going?

Tenerife.

I'm going to Palma.

We've been there before and had a wonderful time.

Oh.

Example C

Are you taking a holiday this year?

Yes.

Where are you going?

Tenerife.

I couldn't park my car and left it streets away – you know parking is getting so much worse; it drives me up the wall. Britain seems to have employed a new army of traffic wardens and as for the congestion charge, everywhere there are empty meters and traffic wardens ready to pounce.

Do you like the wine?

Yes, it's very nice.

Isn't that Fred Kimble over there?

Yes, I must go and speak to him.

Imagination is a wonderful quality and a great human attribute, but it can also be detrimental to effective communication. Think of a journalist attempting to read between the lines when interviewing a politician who will not give a direct answer to a direct question. The journalist, and consequently his or her readers, might easily get the wrong message altogether, thus rendering the initial communication negative rather than positive.

The way to avoid this and establish effective communication is very simple – say it how it is. Don't be evasive, don't skirt the issue, don't let your imagination run away with you.

A positive answer will generate a positive response.

The same principle applies to listening. Listen well and respond positively. For example, a positive response from Communicator 2 to Communicator 1 about Polly's telephone number might be 'Do you want me to phone her immediately?' or 'I can't phone her right now, but I'll do so as soon as I can.' This is a far more positive response than the one described earlier in this chapter. The best response of all would be 'Thank you so much.'

So use your imagination positively. Try to visualize the best; imagine that people are going to be pleasant rather than hostile; see the good, not the bad. Always remember that negative imagination causes communication breakdown.

Banish Negativity

Negative thoughts and negative reactions are the biggest destroyer of success, potential success and happiness. A tremendous amount of harm can be created by what people say to one another and what they think – about others as well as themselves. Negative communication prevents us from having positive relationships and creating greater success.

Negative thoughts and negative communication will hold us back from achieving more.

So just reflect on how you communicate with your friends, family, customers, people at work. Are you generally negative or positive? By constantly reacting negatively to someone, and/or persistently criticizing them, you can destroy not only your relationship, but also that person's self-esteem. The effect can last a lifetime!

Equally destructive is the way you think when you say to yourself 'I'm no good at this', or 'I can't cope with that', or any other negative thoughts you might have. You are simply preventing yourself from achieving more. So think positive!

It's worth emphasizing again that negative thoughts and negative communication are the great destroyers of relationships. This book is about communicating to win – just reverse that destructive human characteristic and see the staggering results you will achieve.

Pocket Reminders

▥ Concentrate on listening
▥ Do respond, don't react
▥ Control your imagination and use it effectively
▥ Think positive and be positive – today and every day.

Wise Words

Before you put someone in their place you should put yourself in theirs.

Author unknown

3

Helping People to Like You

In order to be an effective communicator it is an advantage to be liked rather than disliked. There is no need to go to extremes by trying too hard to be liked – you cannot please all of the people all of the time. The important thing is to be as natural as possible.

Throughout this book we are looking at how to interact effectively with people and create sound relationships. To do this, one of the objectives must be to win more friends and eliminate any atmosphere of tension, distrust or hostility. You do not have to be patronizing to achieve this – simply bear in mind that one of the laws of success states that what we hand out in life we get back, and remember the saying 'If you want to cheer up, cheer someone else up.'

Be Friendly

I called into our local post office one day and found the Postmaster himself serving behind the counter, looking bored and fed up with the monotony of it all. His hobby is horses, so I asked him 'How is that lovely mare of yours?' His face immediately brightened into a huge smile, his body language changed and he responded with delight, telling me about his latest success in the show ring. Those few minutes brightened his day. As I was leaving, someone who knew me chided me by saying 'What were you trying to get out of him?' 'Nothing', I replied. 'Absolutely nothing.' We do not have to be so selfish that we cannot bring a little joy to other people's lives without wanting something in return.

Friendliness, like good manners, costs nothing.

Respect Other People's Feelings

There is one very important law of human conduct that will keep you out of trouble, make you many friends and at the same time enhance your reputation as an effective communicator. Break this law at your peril!

ALWAYS MAKE THE OTHER PERSON
FEEL IMPORTANT

One of the deepest urges in human nature is the urge to be recognized and appreciated, both as an individual and by what one has achieved.

Sir David Frost, the well-known TV personality, with whom I worked a few years ago, is an absolute master at this recognition and appreciation. He will always greet people with something like 'Richard – great to see you! How are you?' He will then go on to say something like 'I'm so glad you could come', or 'I've been really looking forward to meeting you'. He never talks about himself, and never releases a confidence, but he is always interested in other people, which is what has made him such a first-class communicator. He has mastered the skill of building up each person he interviews, and consequently draws the best out of the interviewee. Sir David is never offensive or rude, as some interviewers are. He draws the best out of people. At the same time, the most powerful people in the world trust him.

One of the great demotivators for people at work is the situation where they feel unimportant – when the boss doesn't notice them, or, even worse, doesn't know who they are. It is not difficult to remember what is usually a fairly small number of names, and it is important. If you can approach people by name you will automatically help them to like you. You should make an effort to chat to your staff from time to time, praise them, listen to their problems and generally be approachable. By doing this you will earn their respect, and if they respect you they will work for you. If they don't respect you they will merely go through the motions.

> A good boss will always make a point of knowing all his or her staff.

Steve Bennett, the founder of Software Warehouse and jungle.com, received the award for the most successful young entrepreneur in the UK in 1999. At the time he employed some 300 people. On a trip round his warehouse, we stopped off at the manager's office, where he took a phone call from a member of staff who'd had a baby at 4 am that day. What was impressive was that she wanted to speak to her boss. He knew all the details, and arranged for flowers to be sent. Steve had a very loyal team of people, and he knew every one of their names – which is very difficult when it involves so many people.

Be Interesting and Interested

My wife has a friend who we will call Ann, and when they meet, she usually greets her with 'Lovely to see you, Ann, how are you?', to which Ann responds with a catalogue of dramas, crises, aches and pains and so on. This goes on for about 20 minutes. If my wife remarks that she has the beginnings of a cold, Ann will reply with 'Nothing like my cold!'

One day Ann and I were chatting and she said 'You know Richard, I don't think I'm a very interesting person', and I replied 'You're about right'. She asked me what she should do about it, and I said 'Stop going on about yourself all the time, and find out about other people. Ask them about their own worries and concerns and pressures, then you'll be able to compare notes and have a decent conversation. It's very boring when you're so wrapped up in yourself.'

That story illustrates a simple but important point: to be interesting all you have to do is be interested.

> Ask a lot and listen and encourage other people to talk about themselves.

By listening to others and asking questions every one of us can find something in common with someone else, whether it is our work, the place we live, sport, a hobby, a mutual acquaintance or whatever. By taking the trouble to find common ground, we can make communication very much easier.

The essential difference between good and bad conversations is down to the closed question that gets the yes or no answer and the open question that encourages the other person to talk. Now we all know this, but some people find it difficult. So here is a little help.

Open questions to get you under way

- ▓ What happened when you saw her?
- ▓ How could we approach this?
- ▓ Do tell me how you see the situation.
- ▓ Anyway, how do you feel about it?

Encouraging questions to keep the conversation going

▓ Can you tell me a little more about what you actually did?
▓ And then what happened?
▓ Do go on, this is really intèresting!
▓ How do you mean?
▓ In what way?

Useful questions to probe deeper

▓ How did you reach that decision?
▓ What caused that, do you think?

Here are some examples of conversation openers, all prefaced with those wonderful words 'who', 'when', 'why', 'what', 'where', 'how', 'would' and 'which':

▓ Who are the decision-makers within your company?
▓ Who compiles your data at the moment?
▓ Who will be attending the meeting?
▓ When are you looking to implement the new system?
▓ When can we discuss matters further?
▓ When can I call you again?
▓ Why do you foresee a problem?
▓ Why is the price an issue?
▓ Why do you need more time?
▓ What are your major concerns?
▓ What are you looking for in a software package?
▓ What are the key areas of your business?
▓ Where do you see your company going in the next few years?
▓ Where does your analýsis come from at the moment?
▓ Where will the system be located?
▓ How important is this project to you?
▓ How can I find out more?
▓ How would this fit in with your requirements?

■ Would you agree that this system suits your purposes?
■ Would a different day be more convenient?
■ Would you like me to present a case at your board meeting?
■ Which is most important to you?
■ Which system would suit you best?
■ Which one is your favourite?

Keep the Customer Satisfied

These basic principles of communication apply as much to a customer/staff relationship as they do to a management/staff set-up. There is nothing so off-putting as the surly shop assistant, the uncommunicative waitress, the monosyllabic booking clerk/telephonist/receptionist, or indeed anyone from whom you are trying to obtain information or assistance.

Let's use a simple supermarket scenario to illustrate this point. You are looking for a particular product and cannot find it in the place you thought it might be. You ask an assistant where it is. 'Don't know' is the mumbled reply.

Now, your first reaction is probably one of irritation at the assistant's ignorance and lack of help. But when you think about it, the initial fault lies with the store's manager, for his or her failure a) to communicate with the assistant, and b) to teach that assistant how to communicate with customers. It would take very little time or effort to teach the assistant to say 'I'm sorry, I don't know, but I'll find out for you.' As it is, there has been a complete lack of communication between management and staff, which in turn has been passed on to the customer, and which might easily lead that customer to take his or her custom elsewhere in the future.

At the other end of the scale, there is nothing more satisfying than the staff in a shop or hotel who recognize their customers and make a point of being pleasant, polite and helpful. Let me illustrate this with a personal experience.

A few years ago my wife and I spent four days in County Cork, Ireland. We stayed in a small hotel in the town of

Macroom. The hotel itself was nothing special, but the Buckley family, who owned it, were absolutely charming, making us welcome, introducing us to the locals, and pointing out places of interest to visit. A year later we went back to Cork and booked into the same hotel. As my wife walked into the lobby while I parked the car, she was greeted with 'Hello Mrs Denny, how nice to see you again.' Now that was one year later! We were amazed that they remembered us, and we felt very important.

That is an excellent example of the right sort of communication between customer and staff. The hotel in question has since expanded to three times its original size. The owners didn't get that expansion in business due to the quality of the food, or the bedroom furniture, but by how they demonstrated their care and interest in their customers.

Sell Yourself

Career advisors often stress the importance of people selling themselves at an interview, but don't teach them how to do it. It is now widely accepted that, for example, to be an effective salesperson the seller must sell themselves before ever attempting to sell a product or a service, but exactly how is this done?

The answer is very simple – be interested in other people. Ask questions. Listen. Be observant. Find the common ground. By striking up a pleasant and effective communication rapport you are far more likely to turn a potential client into a long-term customer, because that person will both like and trust you.

In the sales world it is true that 'people buy people'. We will buy the person before we buy the product or the service, which is quite right in a marketplace where we have a choice. Politicians, for example, try to sell themselves before they sell their policy, manifesto and so on. Their impact can range from their appearance to the sound of their voice, and research has shown that people will vote for the candidate they like, and not necessarily for what that person says.

To illustrate this further, let's take the examples of two computer salesmen. Salesman C calls on a company for the first time, and pronounces the company's equipment outdated, difficult to service, and insufficient for its needs. His company has all the answers. He is pushy and aggressive and attempts to close a sale there and then. Quite naturally, he is rebuffed.

Salesman B calls, also for the first time. He asks what equipment the company uses and whether people find it suitable for their needs. He speaks to members of staff individually, shows a personal interest, and enquires about any particular problems they may have with that equipment. He suggests that a certain piece of kit might just be the answer to a certain problem. He does not try to force a sale.

When that company does need new equipment, guess who gets the sale? Salesman B has not only sold his company, he has sold himself. Because he has shown an interest and displayed a personal touch, people like him and can relate to him. His interpersonal communication has been excellent.

The same principle applies to someone being interviewed for a job. As well as answering questions, it is important to ask them, to show an interest in the company one hopes to be working for. Here are a few examples of questions that show this interest:

▓ What sort of training do you provide?
▓ When would I get on the first training course?
▓ When did you, sir/madam, start with the company?
▓ How did you progress to your current position?
▓ What were you doing before you joined?

Any question that shows an interest in the company will help your prospective employer to be more interested in you, and thus increase your chances of landing the job.

Interviews

There are numerous books and training programmes on how to pass an interview. Of course there is some value in them, but we have gone from the sublime to the ridiculous. People are becoming so incredibly effective at the interview that all are suffering. What is really happening is that the interviewee is becoming so effective in selling themselves; they are given the job and then find that the job was not what they believed it would be. The employer sells the job too well and they find that the new employee is not what they thought they were. So, many companies now employ a variety of tests such as psycho-metric testing and personal profiling, in an attempt to minimize the square peg–round hole situation. I personally recommend that at a job interview, the interviewer sets the scene very clearly in an attempt to eliminate the mismatch, and the easiest and most effective way is to say something along these lines: 'Yes, of course I'm going to sell you the job, but I'm also going to explain all the drawbacks and pitfalls to get across to you the good and the bad points of this position. I would appreciate you doing the same, because if we get this wrong it is not only very costly for us, but incredibly miserable for you.'

Admit Your Mistakes

Anyone who has the ambition to get on in life is going to make a mistake or two along the way. An error of judgement, the wrong word spoken, an inaccurate calculation – no one is perfect.

Anyone who doesn't make a mistake isn't doing very much in the first place.

Mistakes – even the simplest ones – can lead to conflict and mistrust and consequently to a total communication break-down. To prevent this, be honest. Admit your mistakes. Apologize. Don't lie, don't try to fudge it, don't try to blame someone else. Be upfront about it and say 'I'm sorry, it's my fault'.

By being honest you are immediately doing three things that will go a long way towards rectifying the situation. You are maintaining people's trust in you; you are avoiding conflict; and you are preventing a communication breakdown that would only make the situation worse. You are also, in the longer term, helping people to like you more, because they will admire your honesty.

The same basic principles apply to people in commerce who are attempting to provide a better service and greater customer care, and of course part of that process is handling complaints. We all know the old saying 'the customer is always right', and we also know that some people take this to extremes in order to get something for nothing. Nevertheless, a surprising number of businesses make it extremely difficult for a customer to complain, and when a customer does, the company handles it very badly and tries to defend and justify the poor service or product quality.

I was in a pub once when a customer complained that his beer wasn't 'right'. The landlord scowled, held the glass up to the light, sniffed the contents, took a sip and announced that there was nothing wrong with it, adding that he'd cleaned the beer lines only that morning.

The customer persisted – he seemed to be something of an aficionado when it came to beer – and the landlord grudgingly gave him a fresh pint. The customer drank this, put his empty glass on the bar, and left.

It is very unlikely that the customer has been back to that pub. He might have done if the landlord had been polite, apologized and offered him a different beer from his large selection. As it was, the landlord lost a customer for the price of a pint and his inability to communicate properly.

Going to the other extreme, there is a supermarket chain in

the United States that has the reputation of providing out-standing service and truly backing up its maxim that the customer is always right. On one occasion, after Thanksgiving, a customer returned to the butchery counter with a bag containing turkey, and complained that it was substandard, inedible, and had ruined the family's Thanksgiving celebrations. The butcher immediately apologized, opened the bag, and found nothing but a carcass inside.

The butcher's natural reaction was, of course, 'Come on! If it was that bad how come you've eaten it all?' However, the butcher stuck to the company's policy and responded with 'How can I put this right?' This might explain why market research shows that the average shopper drives past seven other supermarkets to do his or her shopping at this one.

A little humility goes a long way. When you have made a mistake or said something hurtful, admit your error and try to put it right. By doing so you will almost certainly build that relationship, rather than erode it, and you will become a better communicator and develop the trust and confidence that good communication can engender.

If you are a manager or a leader in business, it is imperative that you develop a 'no-blame' culture. If you don't, the consequences are disastrous. If people make mistakes, and having done so fear they will be shouted at or even fired, they will never actually do anything. For too long, during the recession of the 1990s, there was a 'no-decision' syndrome. People were simply not making decisions, and as a result it took longer to get out of the recession. There was a fear that if you made a decision and got it wrong, you would not hold on to your job.

People don't leave companies, they leave people.

If you are a manager or leader, when people make a mistake ask them what they learnt from it, and what they'd do next time. This lets people use their mistakes to develop into more successful individuals.

If you make a mistake, always put your hand up.

Key people sometimes have difficulty in confessing a mistake. If you are like this you must overcome it. You must also be able to apologize, whether it is to your partner or to a business colleague. Being able to apologize will build the relationship, build the communication style, and above all help other people to like you.

Pocket Reminders

- Always make the other person feel important
- To be interesting all you have to do is to be interested
- Use people's names – the sweetest sound
- Be a good news carrier
- Learn to sell yourself
- It's not what you say but how you say it
- If you're wrong, admit it
- Be prepared to apologize.

Wise Words

Your temper is one of your more valuable possessions. Don't lose it.

Author unknown

4

Dealing with People

Many of the frustrations that we experience in life come from dealing with people. How often have we heard the statements 'The job would be great if it wasn't for the customers!', 'The boss is so difficult!', 'I can't relate to so-and-so'? Getting other people onto the same wavelength as ourselves and persuading them to do what we want them to do is one of the most valuable skills in the workplace. Indeed, for any manager it is vital!

Motivate – Don't Manipulate

Effective leaders know that in order to motivate a person it is important to find out what motivates that individual – money, promotion, job satisfaction, recognition and so on. What sort of lifestyle does the individual want? What does he or she really enjoy doing? What are his or her hobbies, pastimes, etc? Having found out the answers, you need to show the individual how to get what he or she really wants.

> The difference between good leadership and poor management is the difference between motivation and manipulation.

Motivation is getting people to do something because they

want to do it: manipulation is getting them to do something because you want them to do it.

Emotional Intelligence

In order to motivate effectively you have to have good communication with an individual, and you also need to be aware of emotional intelligence (EQ).

EQ involves not only understanding and managing your own emotions, but also recognizing emotions in other people so that you can handle relationships. You need to have empathy with other people and also to be self-aware so that you are able to be sensitive to others.

The five characteristics of EQ

▧ Self-awareness – to assess your abilities and your feelings, because they guide your decisions.
▧ Self-regulation – to make your emotions a spur, not a distraction. Self-regulation will also help you to hold out for better results.
▧ Motivation – to provide the fuel that drives you in the pursuit of your goals. You must have goals and believe in them.
▧ Empathy – to win support from others because you have tried to understand how they feel.
▧ Social skill – to enable you to read social situations, to have manners, charm and grace and the quality of leading by example.

> It is essential to have empathy with people in order to understand what motivates them.

The most important aspect of effective communication is the ability to stimulate enthusiasm in others – from your own enthusiasm, the way you speak, the tone of your voice and your body language. Genuine enthusiasm is irresistible and very persuasive. We are all drawn to people who demonstrate passion and enthusiasm, be it on TV, radio, face-to-face at meetings, parties or wherever. Enthusiasm is like a magnet.

Praise where praise is due

There is nothing like a word or two of praise to make someone feel good and maintain their enthusiasm, and consequently their performance in the workplace. Too often people are quick to find fault, to criticize and carp. They have a totally negative attitude which kills ambition, destroys confidence and erodes creativity.

Criticism is only acceptable if it leads to positive communication that will eliminate errors and enhance performance. So instead of saying, for example, 'That design is awful; it won't do at all', try saying 'I can see how you're thinking, but have you considered this approach...?'

Criticism is only acceptable if it is constructive.

We all feed good when someone congratulates us on a job well done. Our confidence grows and our self-belief is enhanced. Just as important are our feelings about the person who has delivered the praise: inevitably, the relationship will have been reinforced.

Nevertheless, remember that praise and compliments must be deserved and sincere. And do distinguish between praise and flattery. One of the best definitions of flattery is telling other people what they already think about themselves.

Praise is sincere; flattery insincere.

An obvious example of the amazing effects of praise is something that parents do naturally with their children. Parents want their baby to smile, so what do they do? They smile and keep smiling until the baby smiles. Immediately they get a smile, the delighted parents demonstrate loads of enthusiasm and praise, and the same sequence is repeated through all the stages of baby development – crawling, standing, walking and so on. Parents develop a 'you can do it!' attitude towards the child, thus encouraging his or her progress. Then, when the child is mobile, praise appears to decline and the negative takes over – 'Don't touch', 'Don't go too far away', 'Don't go there', etc.

If we are really honest, we should acknowledge that in our daily lives we neglect to give praise, for example to a partner for some kindness, or a child for some achievement at school. We are so wrapped up with ourselves and our own pressures that we forget to show appreciation to a colleague or family member. Without doubt, giving praise and appreciation helps other people's self-development, and is a guaranteed way to help us to become better communicators.

The distribution of praise and criticism brings us back to EQ and the importance of being able to empathize with every member of your staff – or, if you are a member of that staff, with your boss. Feeling empathy is absolutely vital if we are going to achieve effective communication, and therefore quality performance.

So always bear in mind that every member of your staff is an individual, not a robot, and be aware of each one's quirks and characteristics and way of doing things. Don't try to crush the cocksure, headstrong individuals who think they know it all – give them their head from time to time, but don't let the reins out too far; give them praise, but don't let them think they're invincible. And if you have someone who is shy and unsure, but shows potential, give encouragement; make that individual know that he or she is a valuable member of the team.

Whoever you are dealing with, make sure that you can empathize with them. Identify each person's good points and shortcomings, then develop the former and reduce the significance of the latter through effective interpersonal communication.

Honesty

Without doubt, giving praise, appreciation and encouragement is a sure way to get the best out of people and at the same time to become a better communicator yourself. One certain way to reduce people's perception of your ability to communicate is by being dishonest.

Does a particular salesperson give you a confident or safe feeling because he or she is honest, telling you the way it is? Do your colleagues feel they can trust you? Does your boss trust you? Honesty and integrity are winning qualities, and they are also major attributes of the effective communicator.

The 21st century is creating huge opportunities for us all to live longer, play more, travel more and achieve greater financial security. It will also see a revolution on some of the bad communication practices which became so prevalent towards the end of the 20th century – the spin, the soundbite, the innuendo – all of them under the banner of misinformation that became associated with governments and large corporations. Misinformation can only lead to communication breakdown and negative attitudes, and should be avoided at all costs.

Assertiveness

Now comes that rather frustrating A-word: assertiveness. Some people cannot master being assertive and others have mastered it to such a degree that no one does anything until the master assertive barks.

Saying 'No'

One aspect of being assertive involves being prepared and able to say 'No'. Now, some people are always saying 'No' – it's one of their favourite words – and these people achieve very little. On the other hand, a person who cannot say 'No' becomes unable to cope, and consequently unable to perform or achieve effectively. This leads to excuses, a defensive attitude and stress. These people are also indecisive and in the long run will lose the trust and confidence of those who live and work with them.

Being assertive does not mean that you have to be overbearing, domineering or dictatorial.

To say 'No' is really very easy. Just say it, when you really feel you cannot or do not want to. In many cases, you don't even have to justify your response or give an excuse. There is a story about a man who asked to borrow his neighbour's lawnmower. His neighbour replied 'No, I'm sorry, you can't.' 'Why not?', was the response, to which the neighbour replied 'My mother-in-law's ill.' 'What's that got to do with it?', the man asked, and his neighbour replied 'Nothing, but one excuse is as good as another.'

In communicating at work, saying 'No' usually requires an explanation so that other people will understand your reasons and realize your workload and the pressure you may be under. Remember, though, it's not what you say, but how you say it. 'No I can't because... ' is all very well, but your intonation and facial expression can make all the difference between getting a response or a reaction. Try this out in front of the mirror and see for yourself.

Being willing to say 'No' and saying it in the right way is terribly important.

If you don't say 'No' and then don't act, you let yourself and your colleagues down, with the result that you build a reputation for being unreliable. You cannot build a relationship of mutual respect by always giving in and not saying 'No'. Some people do this because they fear aggression and conflict, and want to be liked, but in the end frustration builds up and they become aggressive, defensive and consequently disliked.

Asking why

In many instances confrontation can be avoided with compromise – let's trade – how can we achieve a win–win situation? Very easily: use that wonderful word that children use to drive their parents to distraction: Why?

Adults simply do not use the word 'why' enough. When used with the right tone of voice and prefaced with appropriate words it is extremely effective and can prevent a great deal of conflict.

- ■ Do you mind me asking why?
- ■ That's fascinating; why do you...?
- ■ I was just thinking, why is this necessary?
- ■ Can I ask, why now?

To have any chance of influencing, you have to find out the other person's thoughts, or agendas, or pressures.

Get into the habit of asking 'Why?'

Whenever there is a doubt or uncertainty about a request for you to act or make a decision, ask why the request has been made. Accept the fact that a lot of people's communication skills are weak or even lacking. As an able communicator, you have skills you can use to help others communicate effectively. You can also draw people out, give them a chance to explain in detail, and help them to share their feelings and emotions. When you understand this, and develop your own personal style, you cannot help but be more able to influence people.

Be direct

Some people believe they are communicating when they drop hints in a roundabout way and hope the other person is getting the message. This is not the way to deal with people and it very rarely works. In most cases the hint is not even taken, and even if it is it quite often gets the opposite response from that intended, because the other person thought you were getting at something totally different. It is a very negative way of communicating.

Act on advice

Another negative way of communicating is asking for advice and then never acting on it. If you do this constantly, the person whose advice you have sought will come to feel inferior and worthless. It can also lead to frustration. The sales director of a large company once told me 'I always listen to what my reps have to say, then I do the opposite'. One of those reps, who overheard him, later said 'Yes, that's exactly what he does, and as a result we never have enough product to sell!' This particular company had an extremely high attrition rate, and constantly hiring new people cost them a fortune.

In summary, remember that everyone has their individual characteristics and needs to be treated accordingly. Bear in mind the importance of EQ, apply it properly, and your communication skills will improve accordingly.

The way you deal effectively with one person will not necessarily apply to the next one.

Pocket Reminders

■ Find out what people want
■ Show them how to get it
■ Everyone wants to be appreciated
■ Enthusiasm is irresistible
■ Develop your emotional intelligence
■ Praise works: flattery gets you nowhere
■ Be willing and able to say 'No'
■ Say it how it is.

Wise Words

Failure is not a crime. Failure to learn from failure should be.

Walter Winston

5

Giving and Taking Instruction Effectively

It is very rare to come across a good leader of people who is unable to take instructions from others. However, many people who have been given the responsibility of leadership and management make a complete hash of it; and in the vast majority of cases they do so because they are incapable of following other people's instructions.

Taking Instruction

Responding to other people's instructions is quite straightforward provided you are aware of the following:

- what is expected;
- why it is needed;
- when it is needed.

If you are unsure about any aspect of the task, ask questions.

There are a few exceptions to this. A soldier, of course, does not question the orders of his superior unless he wants to get into serious trouble. Similarly, if the navigator of a rally car tells the driver that there is a 45-degree sharp right-hand bend coming up in 100 yards, the driver does not question this, or the car will end up off the road.

Consider another example, this time demonstrating a child's absolute trust in its parents. A family on a country walk was crossing a railway line when suddenly a train was heard. It was almost on top of the family when the mother told the young child to lie down between the lines and keep absolutely still. The parents jumped to one side and the child did what it was told: the train passed directly over the child, who was unscathed.

These are perhaps rather extreme examples, and on the whole we are no longer living in an age where people in the workplace are expected to blindly follow what is demanded of them. Asking questions will lessen the chance of making errors, and reduce the occurrence of the eventual excuse 'but I thought you meant...'

When asking questions, take care not to appear confrontational.

Feedback

Having received the instruction, there now follows the process of carrying it out. The effective communicator will keep the manager/leader updated about progress – in other words, give him or her feedback. Don't wait to be asked; it is much more effective to keep your boss informed, but don't overdo it – if you give feedback at every opportunity, your boss will probably find this intensely irritating.

The effectiveness of feedback can be compared to a modern aircraft's autopilot, which works on the basis of error correction: it is correcting itself on the basis of going off-course. It is important for everyone in business to have accurate information as to where they're going wrong, because that gets them back on the right course.

Clearly, failing to give feedback when something is going wrong will not only jeopardize the job, but also engender mistrust.

An effective leader is willing and able to hear the bad news as well as the good.

We have all heard the expression 'don't shoot the messenger', but unfortunately there are a lot of managers who let themselves down by ranting and raving at the bearer of bad news, regardless of who or what is to blame. The upshot of this is that people are afraid to speak up when things are going wrong, resulting in a communication breakdown. 'Shooting the messenger' is a sign of weak management. The correct thing to do when faced with bad news is to view the news positively. Look at it as an opportunity for improvement, a mistake that can now be prevented, or even just a learning experience. Whenever I'm faced with a negative situation I react and then respond. Firstly, I allow myself some time to come to terms with the frustration or misery and then respond by saying to myself 'How can I turn this to my advantage?' So, therefore, be a responder and be proactive:

■ Identify the problem.
■ Put it right.
■ Make sure it doesn't happen again.

Recriminations will only lead to ill-feeling and mistrust.

Dealing with Problems

Dealing with problems at work in a positive manner is a vital part of business communication and helps to engender a productive environment. People must be able to say what they think and be able to share the good news as well as the bad. The expression 'we all learn from our mistakes' is absolutely true, so long as we face up to those mistakes. No matter who we are or how good our track record is, we are not going to get it right every time.

When I take on a new member of staff I stress the importance of two-way communication. I always say:

If you are not happy, please tell me; if you are unsure, please ask; if something goes wrong, please come and discuss it; if I say something that upsets you, please don't bottle it up – come and talk, and we'll solve it. I am not a mind reader, so if anything whatsoever causes you to feel unhappy, unsure or stressed, it is up to you to let me know.

This is the right attitude for managers to take in any organization, however large or small, in order to maintain effective personal communication at all levels, and minimize the risk of mistakes, misunderstandings and ill-feeling. Failing to communicate problems leads to stress and mistrust, affects performance, and can cause a total communication breakdown.

Bottling up a concern or a grievance is quite the worst thing an individual can do.

Internal Politics

It is sometimes said that all large organizations have internal politics. This may be true, but it should not be excused. If you are in control, do everything you can to make sure you are not creating an environment where internal politics fester. And if you're not in control, do not be party to them.

Internal politics not only are damaging to the individual, but can also be detrimental to the organization itself, as in the following case.

In a particular publishing company regular editorial meetings were held, at which editors had to convince the sales and marketing departments that any book they had been offered by an author, and which they liked, could be promoted effectively and sold in sufficient quantities to make publication worthwhile.

Unfortunately this company suffered from an old-fashioned hierarchy system and the heads of departments took the view that the people who worked under them should do as they were told and keep their opinions to themselves. In other words, positive communication was not encouraged.

On one occasion a book came up for discussion and some of the more junior members of staff were enthusiastic about it. The marketing director immediately put them in their place and persuaded the meeting to reject the book, arguing that the author was unknown and the subject was 'dicey'.

The book was *The Day of the Jackal*. It was quickly snapped up by another publisher. It became a worldwide bestseller, a hugely successful film, and the author went on to become one the world's leading writers of fiction. If only that sales director had been prepared to listen to his staff, rather than regard them as a threat.

This story illustrates just how important it is that senior management should have the support of the workforce, and vice versa. If this is not the case, the business will suffer. Positive interpersonal communication at all levels is essential. I will say it again, people don't leave companies, they leave people.

The Way to Say It

Sir John Harvey-Jones was one of the most famous industrialists in the UK. After his retirement from ICI, he became a much sought-after conference speaker, and his *Troubleshooter* TV programmes were compulsive viewing. One of his great skills is his ability to communicate and the way in which he does it, by imparting constructive criticism without being offensive. Brought in to advise on how to improve a company's performance or streamline its image, Sir John would always advise, never tell.

There is a big difference between advising and telling. The person giving the instructions (or in Sir John's case, possible solutions) has to command the respect of the people under him or her in order to get the desired results.

> The best leaders lead by example, but leadership also involves the giving of instructions.

So ask, or advise, don't tell. Telling, demanding, ordering – call it what you will – is more than likely to get people's backs up, so that they will do the job grudgingly and with the minimum of effort. Nor will it help them to like you. Ask, politely but firmly, and you'll get the results you want. After all, which way do you prefer to be spoken to?

In this section we are concentrating on the face-to-face or spoken communication on the telephone; we will discuss written communication later. So let's run through the process of giving effective verbal instructions:

▓ Leave as little doubt as possible about what is expected.
▓ Explain why the task is needed, so that the person carrying it out knows who or what it is aimed at.
▓ Make clear when it should be completed by.

In some cases you may need to explain how the task should be carried out. However, remember the benefits of delegating, and allow for some creative input from the person concerned. Don't remove the challenge and make the task mundane and boring.

On the other hand, you may prefer to let the person concerned just get on with it, provided he or she feels you can be approached for guidance if necessary. Make sure you monitor any mistakes being made, and always remember to give praise and credit for a job well done.

Don't create a situation where mistakes go unnoticed until it is too late.

Communication Methods to Avoid

Sarcasm should be avoided at all costs in the workplace. Imagine the case of someone who has just had an awful experience in a meeting and has handled it very badly, and a colleague says 'You handled that meeting really well!' Sarcasm is fine among a bunch of friends indulging in a bit of friendly 'mickey-taking' in the pub, but in the workplace it is a very negative form of communication.

Another thing to avoid is talking down to people. It makes them feel insignificant and unworthy, and will lower and perhaps destroy their confidence. Steer clear of phrases such as:

▓ 'I don't think you should be doing that, because you're not qualified.'
▓ 'I'm not going to give you that job, because you haven't done it before.'
▓ 'I don't think you're experienced enough.'

Don't make people feel inadequate. Build them up, and they will rise to your level of expectation.

Here are some useful phrases that can be used to help build confidence:

▓ 'You're good at that.'
▓ 'You're the best person to handle this.'
▓ 'I'd like you to carry this out, because then I know it will be handled properly.'
▓ 'I'm going to ask you to do this because I know I can trust you.'

The ticking off

A manager intended giving a member of her staff a ticking off. The manager called the employee into her office. Later the staff member was asked by a colleague what the conversation was about, and replied 'I haven't got a clue.' Obviously the manager was not communicating clearly. This scenario can be avoided. There is a very straightforward way of ticking someone off:

▦ Be absolutely honest and say what needs to be said, whether it is about BO or attitude. Spell it out.
▦ Keep the meeting completely private – unheard and unseen. Remember the saying 'praise in public, chastise in private'.
▦ Criticize results and performance – not the individual, unless it is a very personal matter.
▦ Show the person how to improve.
▦ Look the person in the eyes when you speak.
▦ Build the person up at the end. Re-emphasize the person's good points, so that his or her self-confidence is retained.

Pocket Reminders

▦ Be clear and specific with your instructions
▦ Follow other people's instructions, but don't be afraid to ask questions
▦ Avoid internal politics at work
▦ Sprinkle genuine compliments liberally
▦ Don't shoot the messenger
▦ Avoid sarcasm and talking down to people
▦ If you have to tick someone off, make sure you do it effectively.

Wise words

The best way to have a good idea is to have lots of ideas.
Bits & Pieces

6

Body Language

It is said that we buy more with our eyes than we do with our ears.

Seventy per cent of all communication is visual rather than auditory.

Effective communicators listen to what other people say, control and manage what they say themselves, but are also aware of the signals their body language gives, and notice other people's body language. This is an essential part of the communication process. It is claimed that every day we communicate with some 4,000 words and sounds.

In the so-called 'science' of body language, it is claimed that there are some 750,000 signals, 15,000 of these from the face alone.

It is hardly surprising, therefore, that body language can be so difficult to define accurately.

So, what can we learn from these statistics? I would suggest that the majority of people can control what they say with only

4,000 words and sounds in habitual use, but if 750,000 signals are involved we cannot expect to fully control the information projected by our bodies. When the spoken word is in conflict with the body language signal, the body language information will invariably be correct because it is spontaneous.

Pitfalls of Interpretation

There are many interpretations of body language, position or movement, and these of course vary according to nationality, culture and behavioural conditioning. Some critics claim that body language is too complex to form the basis for firm assumptions, particularly in a multicultural society. For example, many people regard avoiding eye contact as an indication that a person may be lying, but others might interpret this as a sign of nervousness or insolence. In some cultures direct eye contact is seen as a challenge to authority and it is regarded as polite to look away when being addressed by a senior figure. Engaging in eye contact is therefore one example of behaviour that can be misinterpreted in the workplace.

However, there are always exceptions to the rule, and it is important to build your own understanding of people's body language. Develop your own perceptions.

Make the effort to read facial expression and body language movement, and listen consciously with your eyes.

Reading the Signs

It has been claimed that more human communication takes place by the use of gestures, postures, position and distances than by any other method. There are times when people need to control body language in order to communicate effectively;

for example, most extrovert people are tactile, and more likely to touch other people as part of their method of communicating than an introverted person. However, a tactile person can cause great discomfort when touching another, more introverted person. Being touched by another human can cause great offence to some people, although a tactile, extrovert person would have difficulty understanding this.

It makes sense therefore to try to recognize whether a person is an extrovert or an introvert, and one of the easiest indicators is to watch that person sit down. The more introverted person will push the chair very slightly away: the more extrovert person will put up the chair underneath them. The introvert requires space, and never gets too close: the extrovert will come much closer. This is why it is important to listen with the eyes.

Some interesting points about body language

- ▓ Your body language is sending messages all the time.
- ▓ Those messages are sometimes clear and sometimes foggy, but are mostly about feelings.
- ▓ Most people can learn to read the messages with a reasonable degree of accuracy.
- ▓ You can change how you are feeling, by consciously changing your body language.
- ▓ Your preferred body positions convey a message about the kind of person you are.

Awareness of the above creates an opportunity to change if there is a need or if you are not happy with the messages you are conveying. So, do become aware of how you want to appear. Maybe even model yourself on somebody else whom you approve of and, if you need to, change your behaviour to become the sort of person that you really want to be.

Dressing the Part

A great deal of body language communication is subconscious and therefore automatic, but there are some elements that you can control, and as a result communicate more effectively. One of these is your personal appearance.

Fascinatingly, clothes and general appearance have an impact on body language. Have you noticed how people with a new hairstyle sometimes walk differently, or how people move in a different way according to the different types of clothes they are wearing?

How do you dress? What jewellery do you wear? What is your hairstyle? All these will manifestly demonstrate to an observer the person they think you might be. Now, of course, the observer could be completely inaccurate, but nevertheless will form opinions that can be difficult to shake off. The expression 'don't judge a book by its cover' may be true to a certain extent, but equally remember that getting the cover right will dramatically enhance the sales of books in certain markets, because that is usually the first thing that attracts people to it. Conversely, perhaps we should also bear in mind this comment from Charles Dickens: 'There are books of which the backs and covers are by far the best parts.'

It is important to dress for the job you want, not for the job you have. In business it is essential to dress according to the image we wish to present to support our product, industry or the service that is provided. Consider this example: I recently worked at a major British bank and came across a fairly senior member of staff with an outstanding personality, incredible enthusiasm and enormous people skills. However, this man's appearance held back his career progress. He always looked a complete mess – ill-fitting clothes, awful colour clashes, disastrous shoes. In this business environment, his superiors just could not promote him any further because of his lack of attention to his appearance. As the saying goes, 'the right appearance will not necessarily get you into the boardroom, but the wrong appearance will almost certainly keep you out'.

Many people believe it is their right to dress how they wish, and I cannot disagree. However, there is a time to work and a time to play, and while at work employees must conform to their employer's business culture, as customers can and will easily judge a company by the appearance of its employees.

Sign Language

To communicate effectively, it is essential to have at least some understanding of how to read and interpret facial expressions and general appearance. Can you tell when a person is depressed, worried, stressed, lacking in confidence? Can you tell when a person is experiencing problems at home, or when someone is not coping effectively? You should be able to pick up signals from body language that will give you an opportunity to take the necessary steps to find out someone's problems. Take note of signs such as people letting their appearance go, losing or gaining weight, walking as though the cares of the world were on their shoulders.

Also be conscious of indicators that imply that someone may not be telling the whole truth. These are often very straightforward, such as a person replying to a question and at the same time fiddling with his or her watch, scratching his or her neck, rubbing his or her nose, or not looking you straight in the eye. If a person is not sending out the usual signs during a conversation it is possible that he or she is avoiding an issue, or not telling the whole truth.

Watch for body language signals when you are talking to people. If they are running out of time, or bored or not interested in what you are saying, their bodies will tell you. They will become restless, constantly changing position, adjusting their dress, looking around the room, edging towards the door. If people want to hear more, if they want to buy from you, their bodies will tell you. They will look you straight in the eye, pull their chair closer or lean towards you across the table, concentrating on what you are saying.

Isn't it frustrating that these actions are subconscious? Remember that your own thoughts can and will influence your facial expression, and sometimes your whole body language. If you have negative thoughts about a situation or another person, they might be shown in your face. You can, of course, control this with your conscious mind. Masters of communication most certainly will be able to hide their emotions and consciously put on a smiling expression. A smile is much more acceptable than a frown. Also, it is hard to say something nasty when you're smiling, and apparently it takes fewer muscles to smile than to frown, so smiling should appeal to all of us who are lazy!

There is a whole range of books that go into the subject of body language in great detail, but here are some key points from this chapter:

Pocket Reminders

▨ Listen with your eyes
▨ First impressions are the most important
▨ Dress for who and what you want to be
▨ Manage your own body language and facial expressions.

Wise Words

Thinking is the hardest work there is, which is probably why so few people engage in it.

Henry Ford

7

Written Communication

The most dangerous form of communication

There is one simple rule that should be the basis of all written communication.

You must write not so that you can be understood, but so that you cannot possibly be misunderstood.

The written word is more powerful than the spoken word.

Written communication has a long-lasting effect because it can be read over and over again. It can re-ignite joys or bitterness. In my years of consultancy work I have seen the written word cause more aggression, drama and strikes than any other means of communication. The written word, if there is any ambiguity, will always be read negatively.

Although communicating by letter has decreased considerably in recent years, using e-mail, which of course also requires people to spell and use grammar correctly, has increased. In addition, copywriting has become an increasingly sophisticated skill. Therefore, getting written communication right is still vitally important.

Principles

Let's start with the principles of effective business-to-business written communication.

Keep it short

Time is at a premium in the workplace today, so if you want your letter to be read and have impact, keep it short. Most people opening mail in the workplace will first open those envelopes that seem of immediate interest. They will look to see who the correspondence is from, will read a PS if there is one, and will then read the letter itself if it is short. A long letter will probably go to the bottom of the pile.

There are exceptions to this rule, of course. Research shows that direct-mail letters are more effective the longer they are, and if you are conveying information that has been requested, you obviously cannot cut corners for the sake of brevity. However, a normal business letters should be on one side only, have two or three paragraphs, and have three or four lines per paragraph. A letter like this will be read instantly from start to finish.

I understand that the shortest exchange of letters ever recorded was between Victor Hugo and his publisher shortly after *The Hunchback of Notre Dame* was published. It went like this:

Dear Paul,

?

Victor

To which his publisher replied:

> Dear Victor,
>
> !
>
> Paul

Attract attention

In order for your letter to have impact – to stimulate the recipient's attention and be read – the first sentence is crucial.

> The first sentence of a letter must attract attention and stimulate the reader to read on.

In the advertising world it is the catchphrase that draws the eye's attention, in the newspaper world it is the headline. The first sentence of a letter must speak directly to the reader and appeal to his or her interest.

> Your colleague, Mr Jones, suggested I write to you.
>
> Here is some good news!
>
> It's a pleasure to have an excuse for writing to you.
>
> It was great to meet you last week.
>
> I don't know whether you realized it or not...

The bulk of your letter must relate to the recipient. He or she may not really be interested in you, your company, your product or your service.

Many letters start off with various classic statements that can be ridiculous. Possibly the leading example is the statement 'We pride ourselves...' This normally leads into '... on our [service/quality/reputation, etc]'. My reaction to this is 'Oh really? How interesting. So you are all sitting round priding yourselves. But what do your customers think?'

Statements like 'We pride ourselves...', 'we are the [largest/smallest/most successful, etc]' can all be classified as 'So what?' phrases. They often mean nothing to the recipient. They don't benefit the recipient.

> Any form of written communication must demonstrate complete clarity.

When writing, say it as it is and how it is. Make sure there is no ambiguity. Avoid flowery words and phrases. Make sure that you:

■ use short words, not long ones;
■ use everyday words and phrases, not jargon;
■ keep it plain, not fancy;
■ keep it short, not padded.

The idea here is to try to write as you speak – within reason. Communications such as business letters and reports must remain formal, whereas an internal memo can be written in a more relaxed style.

Avoid negative writing

One golden rule of communication is:

Never write negatively.

When the subject is someone's behaviour or performance, no

letters, faxes, inter-office memos, e-mails, notices and so on should be written in a way that could be construed as critical, condemning or complaining – in other words, negative. There are two exceptions to this rule, which will be dealt with later, but first let's look at why it is so important not to write negatively.

A sales manager wrote to one of his salesmen, criticizing the individual's performance – his lack of sales, his approach, his organization and his planning. The salesman received and read the letter just as he was leaving for another day's sales activity.

What do you think his reaction to the letter was? You are right if you think that he wasn't motivated by it: in fact he was upset to the point of frustrated anger, and whether what his boss had written was justifiable is not the point.

So the salesman thought he ought to deal with the situation immediately. He wanted to justify his performance and was prepared with excuses. Instead of leaving for his first appointment, he waited until 9 am and then rang his boss's office. He was told that his boss was away on business for two days, so he left home, was late for his first call, didn't make a sale and now took an extended coffee break while he began to draft his reply. Then he went to his next call, again didn't make a sale and worked on his reply again over an extended lunch break.

This routine went on for the next two days – no sales, little activity, lots of negative thought. This was not the reaction that the sales manager was expecting or hoping for. He had simply not thought about the reaction his negative letter would provoke in the recipient. The purpose of the letter was to change behaviour and improve performance and results, but it failed.

> If you find fault and have cause to criticize, always speak to the individual first.

Once you have given an individual a chance to explain things, you should be able to agree a way forward. Perhaps even more importantly, in a face-to-face meeting you can give constructive advice on how the individual might change his or her behaviour or activity in order to produce a positive result.

One of my first consultancy undertakings was to deal with a company that had terrible staff problems, with unions gaining in power and eventually calling a strike. I discovered that this was all due to one director who had great difficulty with face-to-face meetings. He could not communicate with the spoken word, he would never speak to groups, and he could never have addressed the workforce. Consequently he resorted to the written word, and the final straw came when he posted a notice in the staff canteen announcing that there would be no salary increases for the next 12 months, and that this was not open to discussion. I have to say that my recommendation to the board was that this director had 'passed his sell-by date', as he was adamant that his methods were right, and was unwilling to change.

Now let's deal with the exceptions to negative written communication. If as a manager you have had to correct or criticize an individual, by all means follow it up with a letter. At the end of your private, face-to-face discussion say that you will be putting the points raised in writing, so that you both have a record of the discussion.

The other exception is when someone is under threat of dismissal. You must, by law, put this in writing.

Re-read before sending

Before sending your written communication, re-read it and ask yourself what your reaction would be if you received it.

Always re-read any written communication before its dispatch.

This also applies to e-mail, where the consequences of a badly worded communication can be even worse than when it is in a letter – a letter is usually read by just one individual, whereas an e-mail can upset countless people.

Use key words

There are certain key words that have great power when we read. They will also generate pleasure in the reader, and they will help build a relationship and draw the reader more closely to the writer. These words are often undervalued. They are 'you', 'your' and 'yours'. The reader, of course, reads them as 'I' or 'me', 'my', and 'mine'. They are great words to use, and can't help but concentrate your own thoughts in putting your message across to your reader, and prevent you from talking too much about yourself.

> If you are going to use a PS, make it a very strong, loud benefit statement.

A PS should not be used for the purpose for which it was actually designed, that is, to communicate an afterthought. Use a PS knowing it will be read before the main body of the letter – if it is strong enough it will attract the reader to the letter itself.

When to write

Some people write far too much and waste a lot of other people's time. Only write when necessary, but, that said, bear in mind also that unnecessary letters of praise or congratulations are often the most appreciated.

When did you last send a congratulatory letter or card to someone you didn't really need to communicate with? (Perhaps they had been promoted, or achieved something within the community.) This is one of the best ways of using the written word in communicating to win.

A congratulatory note takes only a few minutes to write.

Be positive

Be really positive in written communication. Let's look at a couple of examples of how one can improve what at first sight appears to be a positive communication.

A customer ordered 1,000 copies of a booklet with her company name printed on the cover. Six weeks later she wrote saying the booklets hadn't been delivered, and cancelled the order. A few days later she discovered that they had, in fact, been delivered, but wrote again saying it was too late to use them, and could she return them for a partial credit. The reply read as follows:

> We are delighted to hear that your booklets have been located. Unfortunately, we cannot allow a part-credit on these, as imprinted booklets are of no value to us on a return.
>
> Your honouring of our invoice number B636 would be greatly appreciated. A copy of the invoice is enclosed.
>
> We regret our inability to be more helpful.

The writer of that letter has tried to be nice, but has not quite communicated effectively. The letter was negative rather than positive. If a customer really wants something, try to avoid an outright 'No', and let him or her down gently. The reply might be reworded as follows:

> We were very sorry to learn that the copies of your booklet were mislaid in your warehouse. I wish we could take them back, or help you dispose of them elsewhere, but unfortunately they are imprinted with your company name.

Has it occurred to you that they could be used for an identical promotion next year? The content is timeless: it will be every bit as good then as it is now.

I'm sorry we can't be more helpful.

Instead of telling customers what they are not entitled to, or what you cannot do, try to tell them the same thing positively:

Negative: Owing to the fact that printing charges are quite high, we have no alternative but to make a slight charge of £2.50 for this booklet.

Positive: Although printing charges are quite high, you can still get this excellent booklet for only £2.50.

Negative: We regret that we cannot comply with your request regarding a supply of literature, as we are in the process of revising all our published material.

Positive: Our literature is currently being revised. As soon as our printer delivers the latest versions, we will send you a supply.

Writing style

Why do we write differently to the way we speak? If you look at the correspondence you receive, you'll notice that the way people write to you is often totally different to the way they would speak to you on the telephone or face to face.

Those in the public sector are perhaps the worst exponents of poor communication. Not only do these people seem to speak a different language from the rest of us, but in a vast majority of cases their written communication is truly appalling. You have probably come across this yourself, and there are books about 'government speak', but let's list some of the phrases that are particularly tired and tedious.

Under the aforementioned circumstances

Attached hereto

As per your letter of the 15th at hand

Would you kindly be good enough to send me

Your cheque in the amount of £150.00

We are this day in receipt of

At your earliest convenience

You might like to think of some of your own improvements to these.

There is also the controversial subject of how to address the person you are writing to. Is it right to address someone as 'Dear', or is this habit a relic from a bygone age? And, after all, you don't start a conversation with the word 'Dear'. You may like to try some alternatives:

Hello Polly

Thank you Richard for your

Good morning Arthur

E-mail is one of the greatest inventions, but it is becoming the world's biggest time-waster. There are numerous stories of people receiving literally hundreds of e-mails a day, people going on a week's holiday and coming back to 20 hours of work in their inbox and maybe only one or two items of importance. Here are a few tips on effective e-mail management:

■ Be careful who you give your personal e-mail address to.
■ E-mail is not a management tool.

■ Talk more, e-mail less – in some organisations people who sit back to back send each other e-mails.

■ If it is your responsibility, e-mail lists should be compiled by job title rather than by name.

■ E-mail is a dangerous form of communication – as I have already said, the written word can be so easily misinterpreted – be careful.

I give my personal e-mail address to only a select few. I am fortunate to be receiving only 10 e-mails per day and they are ones that I want to receive. This does not mean to say that I do not want to hear from my readers or clients – I do – but I am fortunate that I have help and I am therefore able to allocate time to reply personally to every individual who has the courtesy to make contact. So, do make every attempt to manage your e-mail more effectively – make it a time-saver, not a time-waster.

Keeping in contact

Let's now look at specific opportunities to contact people in writing.

Firstly, with Christmas cards. Some cards can be very impersonal – those printed with a company name but with no handwritten signature; and the company cards with a dozen different signatures on them. Let's face it, most of the people signing these cards haven't a clue who they are going to. The cards that most people value are those bearing a signed name and a personal message. Christmas is a great time to be in contact with people and show that you care, so don't waste the opportunity – write a personal message, and, of course, your own signature.

Secondly, with thank you letters. In business we just don't write enough thank you letters, and yet they are a great opportunity to show goodwill. Thank you for your order, thank you for your phone call, thank you for your help, etc. Look for an opportunity to send a thank you letter: they are always appreciated, as well as being a great way to keep in touch.

Now, here is an outstanding idea which is used by a number of business people to demonstrate how much they care about their contacts. They look in newspapers and magazines to find anything that might be of interest to one of their best clients, then post the article to the client with a little note – 'Thought this might interest you.' It is a super way of maintaining contact and demonstrating the caring process, and it only takes a few minutes to do. You cannot do it with every single contact, of course, but you can use it to demonstrate your feelings towards the people you really value. It can build and cement a relationship, and it is a brilliant way of communicating. After all, most of us manage to write holiday postcards, so why not communicate on a few other occasions as well?

And finally, with a letter of recognition. These letters cement relationships, build your reputation for being a good communicator, and demonstrate your care and interest. You might read in a local newspaper or trade magazine that one of your contacts has been promoted, or won a large contract, or received an award in connection with their work. Don't read the story and do nothing; send the person a note of congratulation – you'll be surprised at the response.

> It's not what we know, it's who we know and what *we do* with who we know that really matters.

One of the laws of success states that whatever you hand out in life, you will get back. It also goes on to say there is a tenfold return. Listening to the radio one morning, I heard an interview with one of my contacts, Alan Jones, who was MD of TNT at the time. When TNT first arrived in the UK, my company did a lot of work with them, but I had since lost contact with Alan, through my own neglect.

The day after hearing Alan on the radio, I wrote to him saying how much I had enjoyed the interview. He replied a few days later, saying he was sending me a book about the freight industry which he thought I might find interesting. I replied, and sent him a copy of my first book, *Selling to Win*, which had just been published.

Ten days later I had an order from TNT for 400 copies of my book. You see, none of us knows where that act of thoughtfulness, kindness or recognition may lead us.

Pocket Reminders

▦ Make an impact introduction
▦ Say it as it is and how it is
▦ Always write positively
▦ Re-read before dispatch
▦ Great Words – you, your, yours
▦ Send a congratulatory note to someone today.

Wise Words

Courage is what it takes to stand up and speak. Courage is also what it takes to sit down and listen.

Winston Churchill

8

Telephone Communication

The telephone is without question still the most important tool in the communications field. The internet may have created the opportunity for people to connect with each other more frequently through e-mail, and may have taken some business away from the postal services – indeed, it has become an exciting tool for creating new opportunities – but the field of telecommunications is still a rapidly growing industry. One only has to look at the massive expansion in the sales of mobile phones, and the services they provide, to realize this.

Contact by Telephone

For the vast majority of businesses the telephone is still the first line of contact between customer and business. It is still a tool of fast – indeed instantaneous – communication. In an age where time is at a premium, where instant decisions are essential, it makes sense to remember the importance of using this brilliant piece of communication equipment more effectively.

Person-to-person contact

One of the prerequisites for anyone applying for a job as a receptionist used to be 'a good telephone manner'. Sadly this is becoming less applicable in the modern world of communications, with more and more organizations in the public and the private sector confronting their callers with a recorded voice that gives them options and instructions to press certain buttons for the services they require. In my view this is not the way any company should deal with its customers and clients, and it has led to the modern malaise of 'telephone rage', because people cannot get the answers and information they require from these disembodied voices. This is quite simply unacceptable, and any company that values its customers and wants to conduct its affairs in an efficient and businesslike manner should have a switchboard operator answering calls.

The firm of solicitors I deal with has about 30 partners, and when I telephoned them recently a switchboard operator answered, much to my relief. The person I wanted to speak to was not there, she told me, but could she pass on a message, ask him to call me back, put me through to someone else, or would I like to leave a message on his voicemail? She was charming, courteous and helpful, and saved me a lot of time and the risk of high blood pressure!

Voicemail

If you accept the value of person-to-person communication, be careful with voicemail or answerphone. Of course they both have a role, and answerphones are highly acceptable out of hours or for home use. Voicemail does have a role within certain public sector organisations, but they make the mistake of giving too many options. Just do remember that people much prefer, if given a choice, to speak to a person. If you have a personal voicemail system on offer, please give the exact time of your return and if you say you are going to return the call, do just that.

Voicemail and answerphones are no substitute for a human voice on the other end of the line.

The message is clear – don't put barriers in the way of your customers wanting assistance, advice, prices or information. If they cannot get what they want quickly, they'll go elsewhere. The purpose of a telephone is to enable one person to speak directly to another person, not to be confronted by a series of options, none of which will give the required information.

A good telephone manner

If we accept that the telephone is the first line of communication and business-to-business transactions, and that it is important to speak directly to another person, we must also accept the importance of having a good telephone manner and sounding welcoming to the person who telephones us.

Now you may immediately ask how or why you should sound welcoming to the person who telephones you in the middle of a meal or your favourite TV programme, and tries to sell you double-glazing or life insurance, but only two or three telephone calls out of a hundred will annoy you, and we shall concentrate on the ones that do not.

What do you say when you answer the phone? Are you really welcoming? Do you sound as though you are pleased to hear the other person's voice? Without facial contact, it is important to convey your enthusiasm in the way in which you use your voice. Use expressions such as:

How nice to hear from you.

What a pleasant surprise.

It's great to hear your voice.

These might grate on the cynic, but they immediately start a telephone conversation off on the right foot, and in any case it would be wrong to base the realities of human behaviour on the cynic, the sceptic, the unkind or the negative.

Because effective use of the telephone is based so much on the voice, the intonation of the voice can make a dramatic difference to the way the person at the other end receives the words. So use your voice well. Vary the pitch and the speed at which you speak.

Convey enthusiasm and interest. In this way you will hold the listener's attention.

Another effective way of using the telephone is to smile as you speak. This may sound corny, but it actually works very well: the person at the other end will pick up on your good mood. Try saying a phrase smiling, then saying it when you are serious. The words will sound completely different.

Using the Telephone Effectively

This book is about communication – building and maintaining relationships – and the telephone is a most effective way of doing that. Phone one person at least once a week, even if you don't need to. An old friend, a past contact, a family member you haven't seen for some time: the call could cost you very little and may bring that person a lot of pleasure. Many people grumble that no one bothers to phone them, but remember the law that states that whatever you hand out in life, you get back. So make that call; it can bring pleasure to both you and the person you are calling.

Conversely, don't misuse the telephone. One of the most frustrating time-wasters is the person who promises to phone back, then doesn't. If you say you are going to return a call, do so, even if you are not able to give the decision or information the other person is waiting for. By phoning back you are at least keeping people in the picture, rather than leaving them to wonder what is happening at your end.

The other time-waster is people who refuse to take a call. Sooner or later they will have to speak to you in order to answer your question or make a decision, so why not now? The least they can do is say 'I'm sorry, I can't deal with this now, but please telephone me this afternoon/tomorrow/on Friday, when I will have the information you need.' It works both ways – business can be lost by people refusing to answer the phone or not returning calls.

Pocket Reminders

■ Use voicemail wisely
■ Be enthusiastic and smile on the phone
■ Phone someone today even if you don't need to
■ Always return calls.

Wise Words

Beware of the most dangerous person in business – the articulate incompetent.

Author unknown

9

Meetings

Are You Lonely?

Work on Your Own?

Hate Having to Make Decisions?

Rather Talk About It Than Do It?

HOLD A MEETING

You get to see other people,

Sleep in peace, offload decisions, learn to write volumes of
meaningless rhetoric,

Feel important and impress (or bore) your colleagues

AND ALL IN WORK TIME

MEETINGS

The Practical Alternative to Work

Let's be realistic: often little work takes place in a meeting.
You could argue that a meeting is a useful way of canvassing
the opinion of more than one person, or of making a decision
with which everyone approves, but there are other, better ways
of going about such things. Meetings produce a high concentration of verbal diarrhoea and very little positive action. The

high point of some meetings is a lengthy discussion about when to hold the next one.

> Most of the time taken up by a meeting consists of people talking about what they should be doing instead of doing it.

All that said, meetings are of course a necessity in most workplaces, and they can vary from the one-to-one to the large gathering. And yes, they can be effective; and yes, they can achieve a great deal, provided they are conducted properly. A great way to have a meeting is to hold it in a room with no chairs – it's amazing how quickly people get to the point!

So let's list a few tips on how to use this form of communication most effectively and make all your meetings worthwhile.

Effective Meetings

If you are going to be organizing and/or running a meeting, you should apply the following principles:

1. Decide the objective or objectives before holding the meeting. What exactly do you want to achieve at the conclusion? Whether it is one objectives or several, the principle is the same. If you don't know what you want, how the devil are you going to get it?
2. Prepare an agenda. This makes the meeting easier to control and gives everyone involved the chance to participate, because they will see in advance what is to be discussed and can prepare themselves accordingly. Even more important, an agenda will help to achieve the objectives.
3. Consult those who are attending on what they would like to see included in the agenda. This is good people-

management, prevents meetings over-running, and enables participants to raise the topics that deeply concern them.

4. Do *not* include AOB (any other business) on your agenda. This is a huge time-waster. It enables people to sit right through a meeting before raising a worry or concern. At that stage there is not enough time to discuss it properly and the meeting will end on a negative note. If you apply point 3, AOB should not be necessary.

5. Decide on a finish time as well as a start time and put it on the agenda. You will be amazed at how people will get to a decision or stop talking when they know there is a finish time. It also helps the chairperson to control the meeting.

6. The contents of the agenda should list under each item:

   ■ what is to be discussed;
   ■ why it is to be discussed;
   ■ what it is expected to achieve;
   ■ when the results are expected.

   The purpose of doing this is to eliminate unnecessary discussion and waffle.

7. As the organizer or chairperson, familiarize yourself with each topic on the agenda, so that you can be brief but also helpful.

Chairing or briefing a meeting

In briefing a meeting, give the background and history of the topic under discussion, and the reason for discussing it now. Elicit new facts, detail or information from the people attending, and invite opinion. When chairing a session, always be positive, look for agreement points, ask silent people for their views, and do not under any circumstances allow personal attack.

Do not allow waffle, and keep people on the subject by restating the objective.

The purpose of meetings is to make decisions. Always ensure that once the decision is made, someone is appointed to carry out the necessary action. Give a deadline for this, and do not allow any deferments – these are simply time-wasters.

Remember that the most pointless and frustrating meetings are those with a weak or inefficient chairperson.

Your contribution

Your presence at a meeting does not mean that you are expected to have an opinion on every subject on the agenda, or that you should contribute to every discussion. If you feel strongly about something, voice your opinion. If you have some experience or knowledge, impart it.

Say something when you have something to say. If you don't know what you're talking about, shut up!

However, it would be completely wrong for you to walk away from a meeting feeling 'I wish I had said so-and-so'. Always state your opinion at the appropriate time. Do contribute, play your part, add value, talk common sense. If you stick to these guidelines, everyone will listen when you speak.

Minutes

If you want your meeting minuted, see that this is done by someone who can provide a concise summary of the points discussed, as well as what conclusions were reached, what follow-up action is to be taken, by whom and by when. Ensure that only relevant information appears in the minutes, and that all waffle is cut out.

Circulate the minutes of the previous meeting in plenty of time before the next one, so that everyone has a chance to read them in advance. This will cut down discussion at the meeting itself. Never permit lengthy discussion of matters arising from the previous meeting's minutes – if it is that important, it should be on the main agenda.

Benefits of meetings

A good meeting is one that everyone leaves feeling inspired, invigorated, re-enthused, knowing exactly what to do and when to do it, and excited about the challenge ahead. If a meeting has been a success, you should leave it thinking 'That was a damn good meeting and really worthwhile.' It is up to you to play your part and help achieve the overall objectives.

Pocket Reminders

■ Decide the objective of every meeting
■ Invite contributions for the agenda
■ Never include AOB on the agenda
■ Always include a finish time on the agenda
■ Speak only when you have something to say
■ Ensure that the minutes are clear and concise.

Wise Words

If you want something done, ask a busy person.

Author unknown

Ten Great Tips for Better Communication

1. Speak to people.
2. Smile at people.
3. Address people by name.
4. Be warm, friendly and helpful.
5. Be enthusiastic about life.
6. Be genuinely interested in people.
7. Look for the opportunity to give praise.
8. Be considerate of other people's feelings.
9. Be thoughtful and respectful of other people's opinions.
10. Be a great listener.

Part 2

Presenting to Win

Presentation Skills

Presentation skills are a must for all aspiring executives. Whether we like it or not, we live in a society where our culture dictates continuing drive for success, achievement and career advancement. This is where presentation skills have a crucial role to play.

In business scenarios I have seen on too many occasions extremely able and intelligent people in executive positions lose their own confidence and the confidence, respect and commitment of the people they are leading. This happens when they make a weak, amateur and in some cases appalling presentation. The business world today demands and expects professionalism; there is no excuse for a poor presentation. I have seen CEOs, Chairmen and MDs delivering boring presentations to their staff without feeling, passion or commitment.

There is no excuse for a bad presentation. There are a plethora of organisations that offer public speaking courses. The Richard Denny Group, www.Denny.co.uk, is but one that would prevent this unnecessary occurrence. For all aspiring executives, master this skill and you will, without doubt, be equipping yourself for career advancement.

In this section of *Communicate to Win*, we will be covering the most important elements to delivering a presentation, but please do accept that this should not be a replacement for a training course with a specialist trainer. The small investment in yourself could well be one of the best investments you will ever make.

The advice that follows can be applied to a public speech, or a formal internal presentation right through to a vital presentation to potential customers to win business.

In every situation, endeavour to communicate the end result of your subject in the early part of a presentation. This is just downright common sense, but not common. If the members of your audience like the result, they will be so much more interested in what you have to say. In business presentations, don't do what so many amateurs do and spend too much time trying to build credibility by relating in detail the company's history, its client base and its experience – this should take no more than one to two minutes. Remember, you are not selling your company, you are selling what it is capable of doing.

The most important tip which will be repeated in this section is **tell people stories, anecdotes and analogies. If that is all you do, you will always hold your audience's attention.**

Learn to Sell Your Presentation

Public speaking is not a mystical art that a chosen few have been fortunate enough to inherit – nobody is born a gifted public speaker. Some people find it easier than others to give public presentations, but there are few things that instil as much fear in people as having to stand up and speak in public.

This part of the book shows you the principles and methods of effective and persuasive communication. The continual theme will be 'it is not what we say but how we say it'.

To speak effectively in public you must be convinced of the following statement: when people are on their feet speaking to an audience they should be either entertaining or selling but not both. (This does not apply to TV and radio presentations, which work on completely different principles.)

Speaking in public is either an entertaining exercise or a selling exercise.

Let's immediately clarify my understanding of entertaining: it can include stand-up comedy or certain types of after-dinner speech. Therefore, most opportunities for people to speak in public are opportunities for selling rather than entertaining. I am going to be so dogmatic as to say that, having removed the entertaining category, all speaking is or should be a selling process.

The first example of someone speaking in public that normally comes to mind is the teacher. We can probably all remember listening to teachers or lecturers who had incredible knowledge of their subject, but while they were talking to us we became bored and uninterested, our attention wandered and possibly we did not even understand what they were talking about.

Surely it is the duty of those communicators to transfer their knowledge to the minds of their listeners, so that the latter can accept or in some cases argue against the message that is being communicated. The transference of knowledge is most definitely a sales process. It is the duty of educators to gain acceptance of their message from their students, and on acceptance a sales process has taken place.

Think for a moment of all the speeches and presentations you have listened to. The ones you can instantly recall and remember with enjoyment or interest will be those where the speakers were selling the subject they were speaking about, rather than just speaking about the subject.

Pocket Reminders

■ A person speaking to an audience should only be either entertaining or selling
■ All speakers are selling something
■ Good public speakers should be judged by the response and reaction of their audience
■ A salesperson is someone who helps people to make up their mind
■ Techniques for selling and public speaking are based on common sense.

Wise Words

If you want to cheer yourself up, cheer somebody else up.

Bits & Pieces

11

Nervous Tension

If you have never spoken in public before, you may dread the thought of it. Perhaps you have kept your head below the parapet until now to prevent the opportunity to speak in public arising or the invitation being presented. Why? Almost certainly because of the fear of failure, which, in turn, can lead to a subconscious fear of rejection and possibly the feeling that you are going to make a fool of yourself. These fears can be summed up as a lack of confidence.

If you have had a bad experience of public speaking, you will almost certainly have experienced a crisis of confidence and may even, albeit dangerously, have classified yourself as one not cut out for public speaking – the experience of failure leads to a lack of confidence, which, in turn, can lead to a feeling of 'I'm no good at that'. You see, we are all conditioned by past experience. Every one of us is born with a positive outlook, but life's conditioning can make some people negative.

Understand Your Nervousness

Taking a simplistic point of view, I would say that there are two types of nervousness that the public speaker should be aware of. The first occurs whenever we have to do something completely out of the ordinary for the very first time – the first sky-dive, the first ride on a horse and the first time we stand up to speak in public. That nervousness can perhaps be described as a feeling of utter terror. This feeling doesn't last and the more times you do what you are afraid of, the more the fear lessens. Remember that outstanding quotation 'The only way to conquer fear is to keep doing the thing you fear to do.'

The second form of nervousness is extremely important and it must be mastered and harnessed by the public speaker. You will certainly have seen or listened to an interview with a well-known actor, where the interviewer says 'You have been on the stage now for many years. Do you still suffer from stage fright or nerves?'

What does the actor say in reply? Invariably it is something along these lines: 'Yes, and you know it never gets better'. The actor may go on to describe his or her nervous tension. Some actors feel unable to speak to their colleagues, others become irritable, some feel physically sick, and some suffer from loose bodily functions!

So, what can we learn from them? This form of nervousness is a natural reaction. The actors are so intent on giving their best that their nervous system sets the adrenaline running and creates an uncomfortable feeling of nervous tension.

Adrenaline and nervous tension are essential parts of a good performance.

Therefore, you shouldn't worry about feeling nervous – quite the contrary: you should worry when you are not feeling nervous, because if that is the case you will not be about to give your best performance.

Dealing with Nervous Tension

Some people find that when they start speaking in public their hands shake, they feel as though their legs are trembling and their voice is quivering. There are, of course, genuine extreme cases, but the vast majority of speakers who think that this is happening to them do not realize that it is never noticed by an audience.

> Take one or two deep breaths just before walking forward or standing up to give a presentation.

After 20 years of speaking at conference, conventions and seminars throughout the world, I have found that a few deep breaths will help master nervous tension before and during the early stages of a public speech. Holding your hands together or grasping the lectern will help if you are shaking. But above all else it is the planning, preparation and practice of your presentation that will build your confidence and help you to overcome the tension.

Pocket Reminders

- To be a good speaker you must understand your fear
- Nervousness can come from terror or 'stage fright'
- The only way to conquer fear is to keep doing the thing you fear to do
- Adrenaline and nervous tension are essential parts of a good performance
- Deep breathing or exercise can help conquer the tension
- Nervous tension is like stress – good as long as it is managed.

Wise Words

Fear defeats more people than any other thing in the world.

Ralph Waldo Emerson

12

Preparation

Confidence comes from thorough and accurate preparation.

How to research and prepare

The more effort you put into the preparation, construction and writing of a talk, the greater will be the enthusiasm about and enjoyment of your presentation.

Stage 1 – Prepare a file

Open a file or get a large envelope and write on the outside the details of the event and preferably, if you know it at this stage, the title of your talk.

Stage 2 – Collect ideas

During the time leading up to when you actually write your speech, use the file or envelope to collect material that could be used. For example, you may be reading a newspaper article that gives relevant facts and figures or suggests a new line of thought. Cut the article out and put it in your file.

Stage 3 – Decide your aims

Before actually putting pen to paper to write your talk, you must decide exactly what reaction you want your speech to have. If you don't know what you want, the audience won't know either. Do you want your audience to:

■ applaud;
■ make a decision;
■ take immediate action;
■ accept your message unanimously;
■ be hostile;
■ be bored;
■ be enthusiastic;
■ laugh;
■ cry?

Maybe you just want your audience to assimilate and understand your message.

Interestingly, you will find that once you have made a decision about what the purpose of your speech is, the actual writing and delivery of it become that much easier. If you know the desired reaction, the action somehow becomes automatic. One of the basic philosophies of achievement is first to decide what you want; then, the stages to get what you want are not really difficult. Remember the old cliché: a person who is going nowhere normally gets there.

Stage 4 – Write a speech

Let's now look at the basic construction of all speeches. Every speech should have:

1. An opening.
2. A message.
3. A close.

Firstly, when writing the speech, list in any order the thoughts, ideas and materials that you have already collected in your file or envelope, and any others that come to mind at this stage.

Secondly, from that list select a sequence of items that follows a logical thought process. This will make it easier for you to deliver the speech and for your audience to understand it.

Thirdly, you can write down the details of each item listed. If it suits your personality, write the complete presentation as if you were going to read it, with paragraphs, sentences and punctuation.

Remember that speeches or presentations should not be read line by line unless they are of a highly delicate nature where meaning can be misinterpreted, for example political statements or chairmen's statements at AGMs. In most cases, therefore, it is so much more effective to speak in the way I have already described; but that said, if you do have to read a speech, practise it well. Use your voice with pauses to make it more interesting; be loud and then be soft; give real emphasis on words of importance; and maintain eye contact with your audience as much as feasibly possible. The preparation of that speech and its layout on your speaking aid will also have an impact on its delivery.

Stage 5 – Prepare your notes

Remember that these notes are your speaking aid and must not be allowed to become a trap.

From your full written text, take the theme of a paragraph and make that a main heading. Then jot down one or two words from the sentences to remind you of the detail or the theme, so that your speaking aid ends up with just headings and sub-headings. It is essential that these are in large writing. Use capital letters and make sure there is a good space between each line. You can identify your main themes with different coloured pens, you can underline, you can 'box in' certain words and phrases, and you can use highlighting and asterisks.

They all make your speaking aid more successful. Whether you are using a series of foolscap pages or cards, make sure that each is numbered at the top.

The acid test that will tell you whether your notes are going to be an aid or a trap is to stand three feet away from them and see if you can clearly read what you have written.

Stage 6 – Practise

Practising your presentation is probably the best way to ensure that everything will run smoothly when you do it for real. Becoming familiar with presenting your material will build your confidence, and will help you with the speaking time. When you practise, your talk may take 10 minutes; when you come to deliver it, it most certainly won't – it could be longer or shorter, but you will soon know whether you speak more slowly or faster in the live occasion, but just remember it is an unforgivable sin in public speaking to over-run your allocated time.

'Drying up'

One of the biggest fears for an inexperienced speaker is that of 'drying up', or forgetting what to say. There are two major causes of this. The first is having no notes because you believe you can speak 'off the cuff' or because you have memorized your speech. There are very few people in the world who have a sufficiently good memory to speak without notes and enough confidence to expose themselves to the risk of a memory lapse during a public presentation. I do not recommend relying on memory – my best advice is never, under any circumstances, speak without a speaking aid.

Pocket Reminders

■ Confidence comes from preparation
■ Remember the six stages of preparation:
- Prepare a file
- Collect ideas
- Decide what you are aiming for
- Write the speech
- Prepare your notes
- Practise
■ Speeches should not be read.
■ Remember that you are speaking for your audience's benefit

Wise Words

Only the prepared speaker deserves to be confident.

Dale Carnegie

13

Content

We have already seen that the basic construction of all presentations is an opening, a message and a close. In this chapter, I will illustrate a number of examples of how to open a presentation, and what to include; but first, a story.

There was a man who owned a donkey, but unfortunately it was untrained and had terribly bad habits. The man found he could do nothing with it. So he looked in the *Yellow Pages* and telephoned a donkey trainer. He explained his problem and asked about the cost of training, and they agreed that he should take his donkey to the donkey trainer's premises.

When he arrived, he once again explained his donkey's bad habits. The donkey trainer said he would start the training process immediately and the owner asked if he could stay on a while to watch and see what the trainer did. 'By all means', replied the trainer. 'Hold on to your donkey'. He then walked across his yard into a shed and came out carrying a large wooden mallet, went straight up to the donkey and hit him with one sharp blow on his forehead. Naturally, the owner was distressed and said 'What on earth are you doing?' The trainer replied 'The first stage of training is to attract his attention.'

It's the same when you speak to an audience – the first stage is to attract their attention.

Attracting the Audience's Attention

Let's describe a few ways in which this can be done:

■ **Make a desire-type statement** – say something that everybody wants to hear. This must of course be totally relevant to your presentation and to the audience. Here are a couple of examples:

'Ladies and gentlemen, during the next 30 minutes I want to discuss some ideas that could dramatically increase your income.'

'Ladies and gentlemen, during the next few minutes I would like to show you a formula that could considerably reduce your expenditure and save you a great deal of money over the next few months.'

■ **Use extraordinary facts.** Using an extraordinary fact about an ordinary subject can be a great attention-grabber. *The Guinness Book of Records* can be a fine source of irrelevant information that can nevertheless stimulate an audience to think.

■ **Use visual aids.** You can produce an exhibit or, if you are using an overhead projector, a stimulating slide. We will cover the use of visual aids in more detail in Chapter 15.

■ Set the theme of your presentation – by reading a text, a statement or a quotation.

■ Tell a humorous story. This method is very common but is certainly not the best, so I include it as a last resort.

Constructing Your Presentation

It goes without saying that every presentation is different, so we will not go into lengthy detail about the exact structure and content of a speech. Instead, let's stick to the principles. Your speech must have:

1. an opening;
2. a message;
3. a close.

You must:

1. present your facts;
2. argue from them;
3. appeal for action.

1. show something that is wrong;
2. show how to correct it;
3. ask for cooperation.

One message at a time

Most speakers find that when they are writing or even delivering their presentation they try to cover too much material.

As a guideline, in a short talk of less than five minutes, you should only attempt to cover one or a maximum of two main points. In a longer talk of, say, 30 minutes, try not to cover more than four or five ideas.

Persuading People to Listen

Many people ask for the best way to get an audience to listen to and enjoy a speech. There are two essential recommendations: exploit the power of pictures; and relate the content to the audience. A third way is to tell a true story.

Use 'picture power'

There is an old saying 'people buy more with their eyes than they do with their ears'. This is why it is very effective to have some visual support when speaking to an audience. However, if this is not possible, or not suitable, you can be even more effective by creating word pictures – or using 'picture power' to get the audience to see by using their imagination as well as to hear. The following two examples show the importance of descriptive communication.

Example 1

Let's say you decided to go skiing for the first time. Helped by a travel agent, you would decide your budget and choose a resort. The next stage would be to purchase or hire some equipment. You would choose a ski suit, which could be a one-piece or a two-piece chosen from an amazing selection of materials, colours and styles. You would need to choose your skis. The correct choice of skis is normally governed by your physical height, although there is a tendency at some ski resorts for people to learn on shorter skis. Again, there are different materials that the skis can be made from with varying flexibilities and breaking strengths. You would now need to choose your ski poles. You could have a straight ski pole or one with a bend at the end. These are always governed by your physical height. Finally, and most importantly of all, comes the selection of the ski boot...

Example 2

Once you have arrived at the resort and been equipped with clothing, skis, boots, etc, it is natural to want to get onto the mountain as quickly as possible. This is often done by taking a cable car, which can be a wonderful experience in itself. As the cable car moves silently up the mountain, the wooden timbered houses with their overhanging eaves form a magnificent sight. Your attention is then drawn to the majestic sight of the trees – pines and conifers that seem to be enveloping you. And then suddenly everything is obliterated from view as the cabin goes into the cloud. When it emerges you have a completely new view – you can see the tops of the mountains and the sun sparkling on the snow. The cable car comes to a halt. You get out, put on your skis and start to move across the snow. The sheer feeling of exhilaration, the crispness of the air and the sound of the skis on the snow – marvellous!

Most speakers spend a large part of their presentation rabbiting on about the subject and then at the very end they get around to the benefits, the object, the purpose or the result. Only then do they describe what it would be like if everybody followed up or took action on what they have been talking about.

The importance of talking about the result cannot be stressed enough. Build a picture of the result. Sell the result. Get your audience to want the result. The how, why, what and when to achieve it then become acceptable and easy to communicate and the audience will be interested.

Relate the content

The second recommendation about holding the attention of an audience is to make sure that the content really does relate to the audience. Some speakers make the error of talking either above or below their audience. They do not communicate with their audience. When you are selecting the content of what you want to communicate you must make sure that it relates to the majority of those listening to you.

Tell real-life stories

The third recommendation for holding attention and also for maintaining a high level of interest in any audience, is to use real-life true stories, anecdotes and analogies. This really is the golden tip for all truly effective communicators. Never make up stories and pretend that they are true.

Whenever a speaker is telling a true story, the audience will be really interested.

Ending the Presentation

There are, of course, countless ways in which a presentation can be drawn to a conclusion. Some are listed below, not in any order of importance, but purely as possible ideas for different occasions.

■ Summarize the main points – except in a talk of less than six minutes, when this would make the presentation far too repetitive. Summarizing can be really effective for presentations where there is a fair amount of detail in the content that needs repeating or re-emphasizing.

■ Appeal for action: 'Let's get going', 'Let's unite'.

■ Pay your audience a sincere compliment.

■ If you are confident enough to carry it off, tell a joke or story to raise a laugh.

■ Use a quotation or a verse of poetry. Choose your material carefully – obviously, if you were making a highly technical presentation to a group of directors in a boardroom, you would be unlikely to close with four verses of Wordsworth!

■ Use good vocal technique to build a climax. You might decide to become very loud or, on the other hand, very soft, or to speak very fast or very slowly.

Pocket Reminders

- The basic construction of all presentations is:
  - An opening
  - A message
  - A close.
- First attract the audience's attention
- Be very familiar with your first two or three minutes
- Explain your theme
- Only deal with one main point at a time
- Use picture power
- Use real-life stories
- Relate the content to the audience

Wise Words

The greatest of all faults is to be conscious of none.
Thomas Carlyle

14

Your Audience

How to Hold Their Attention

We have looked at how to attract the audience's attention, and, of course, a speaker then needs to hold that attention. I have been told that an audience is able to maintain concentration for a maximum of 20 minutes. It is difficult to know whether this is true, but throughout my speaking career, I have tried to take my audience off the subject every 12–15 minutes in order to avoid losing their attention. The techniques for maintaining concentration are some of those we have just been highlighting – namely, tell a real-life story, or use an anecdote or analogy.

> The real secret of maintaining an audience's attention is to be enthusiastic.

Being enthusiastic

Let's return to the foundation of all effective speaking: that a speaker should be selling his or her subject, as speaking in public is a sales process. Have you ever been on the receiving end of a salesperson who is not genuinely enthusiastic about his or her subject? Please don't think about some of the artificial, creepy or smarmy salespeople that you have been faced with (there will always be a few) but bring to mind salespeople who are genuinely enthusiastic about their subject. Think of some of the great communicators on TV, enthusiasts who have taken an otherwise intellectual subject and turned it into something of great interest and excellent viewing.

In another area, what is it that distinguishes one of the world's greatest management gurus, Tom Peters, from the thousands of others in the world of academia and business consultancy? Surely it must be the enthusiasm that he demonstrates in the delivery of his subject. This enthusiasm comes through on his TV and video appearances as well as his live speaking engagements.

On British TV, science has become peak viewing as we see botanists, physicists and chemists delivering what could be otherwise construed as mundane subject matter, but their delivery is made with such enthusiasm it makes the subject interesting. I only wish that when I was at school, history could have been made as interesting as it is by the current historians delivering this subject over the networks.

Please do not get the impression that you have to be a raging extrovert in order to be an effective speaker, though most people find that they can be animated when they are talking about something that they truly believe in, and it is that animation which must be maintained in front of an audience.

So it is with being enthusiastic in front of your audience. The first time you give a presentation remember the lovely cliché: 'fake it till you make it'. By the third or fourth time the enthusiasm should come naturally.

Enthusiasm is very infectious. We are all naturally drawn towards people who exhibit this characteristic – whether it is someone we have met at a party or a child bubbling with enthusiasm returning home from school. We want to listen. We want to hear more, and in turn we can catch that enthusiasm. The use of the voice is so important. It helps if it is alternately fast and slow, loud and soft, with an emphasis on certain words.

Removing negative thoughts

If you do a lot of public speaking, there will be times when even though you are enthusiastic about your subject and about the opportunity to present it, before the presentation you experience something that removes your enthusiasm. It could be a crisis at home, a bereavement or even just a letter from the bank manager.

So, how do you remove that worry or pressure from your mind? You can do it very simply and very effectively. Most people completely undervalue the enormous capacity and capability of the human brain. We are all able to control what we think about. If you don't like a particular thought, remove it, take it out of your mind and tell yourself that you don't want to think it.

If you are a photographer, when you receive your prints and negatives back from the processor, you discard those prints that are poorly focused or not up to standard in other ways. We are able to do exactly the same with our mind, so discard that worry or that negative thought.

Pocket Reminders

■ Keep your audience's attention by being enthusiastic
■ Fake it till you make it
■ Discard negative thoughts

Wise Words

It's not what you say, but how you say it.

Author unknown

15

Visual Aids

Visual aids are exactly what they say they are – visuals to aid the speaker when presenting and to aid the audience. The purpose of having something within eyesight of the audience is to make it easy for them to understand the speaker and to assimilate the message that is being delivered. Many speakers make too much of the visuals and in the process lessen the power of their spoken word.

The equipment normally available for visual aids includes a flip-chart, an overhead projector, slide projector, video projector and, of course, PowerPoint. If a flip-chart is used it should always be positioned for a right-handed speaker on his or her left-hand side. Anything that is written on a flip-chart that is pre-prepared must be professionally done. Any speaker can get away with writing, even though it may not be the best writing in the world, if it is done there and then in front of an audience.

Keep Visual Aids Simple

The most common mistake made by speakers is creating too much material on a visual aid, whatever the visual may be. It is extraordinary how many speakers are tempted to put too much content onto their visual aids, too many words that the audience cannot read. More speakers get into trouble, and more drama and more uncomfortable situations are created in presentations, because of this error than almost any other.

The use of PowerPoint is increasing, and so therefore are situations where speakers are left high and dry when the computer goes wrong or they press the wrong button and can't get back to where they are. A good recommendation is to never be dependent on your visual aid, and always have secondary back-up if you are going to use PowerPoint. A PowerPoint display is not and should not be a presentation. It should just be a visual aid, but unfortunately this is often not the case, and for many audiences a presentation using PowerPoint is becoming something to dread.

Arrive early at the venue, and allow plenty of time before your speech starts to check your equipment, and your visuals – make sure that everything is in order and check that the sequence is going to run well. Lastly, whatever you do, once you have displayed a visual aid don't keep looking at it. It is very common for speakers to keep their eyes fixed on their visual aid, with everyone in the audience looking to see what the speaker can see that they cannot.

Speak to the audience, don't speak to the visual aid.

Pocket Reminders

- Arrive early and check out the venue
- Test all equipment in advance
- If you have to turn your back on the audience, keep talking
- Don't be dependent on visual aids
- Keep visual aids simple
- All visuals must look professional
- Preparation and practice prevent disasters

Wise Words

You can make more friends in two months by becoming interested in other people than you can in two years by trying to get the other person interested in you.

Dale Carnegie

16

Your Appearance & Attitude

Let's consider a few details that can help to build the respect and credibility you are looking for. If it is appropriate, dressing smartly can make a difference to a presentation, and I believe that all male speakers should wear a suit. Some MDs and chairmen intentionally remove their jacket when communicating with their own people. I find this to be an acceptable attempt to remove a 'them and us' feeling and create greater identification, but it is best used by very senior people. Minor details should not be forgotten because they can cause a distraction – a tie that is out of place, for example. Hair should be properly groomed, shoes smart and jewellery should be limited.

Confidence, as we have already said, comes from thorough and accurate preparation, but it can equally be built by having a good outward appearance.

If speakers feel that they look good, their mental preparation and their confidence in their delivery will be enhanced.

Attitude

As well as being conscious of your external appearance, you must also make sure that you are going to speak with the right attitude. And that attitude is of course positive rather than negative.

Many speakers seem to hold a negative self-image just before a presentation. They say to friends and colleagues, or even more dangerously they think, things like 'I'm not looking forward to this', 'I hate public speaking', 'I am just not a good public speaker', 'If I stutter, it'll be a disaster, 'I just didn't have enough time to prepare my speech well' and so on.

These are all negative statements, negative thought processes, and they make it much harder for a speaker to give a good presentation. Instead, you must think positively. Now, I am not saying that you have to go around saying to people 'I am a great speaker' or 'I am really looking forward to this', but you definitely should be saying it to yourself.

Mentally prepare yourself by saying 'I am a good speaker', 'My audience is going to enjoy this presentation'. Visualize your audience enjoying being involved and enthusiastically applauding at the end. See your audience as really nice people.

Say to yourself continually 'It's going to be good, it's going to be great, it's going to be good...'

Pocket Reminders

■ The first impression is the most important
■ Confidence comes from knowing you look the part
■ Don't worry about an accent or a stutter
■ Develop a positive attitude
■ Believe in yourself.

Wise Words

The music that can deepest reach and cure all ill is cordial speech.

Ralph Waldo Emerson

17

Delivery

The speakers walks onto the platform or stands up to begin the presentation. What should happen first?

What do professional speakers do? They pause and cast an eye over the audience with a gentle smile. This relaxes the audience and may even generate a smile in return. There is a Chinese proverb that says 'He who cannot smile ought not to keep a shop'.

Smiling develops a relationship with the audience.

A Speech or a Conversation?

Your speech or presentation has started and you are embarking on what is called 'public speaking', a frightening phrase. Because of our conditioning, it has the wrong connotations.

Someone who sets out to give a public speech is going to deliver the material come what may, regardless of the audience's reaction or feelings. He or she is going to unload the speech on the audience. I prefer the phrase 'a public conversation'. We are familiar with conversations as a two-way process, which is what public speaking should be. The speaker tells the audience how long the speech will last, and delivers the speech, but the audience gives feedback through body language.

Eye Contact

As part of the technique of having a conversation with a group of people, you must make a conscious effort to look into the eyes of your listeners. However large your audience, and even if you are speaking from a platform that is well lit and your audience is in the dark, you must always be scanning your audience.

> Eye contact is crucial to help make it easy for your audience to listen to you.

While we are on the subject of eye contact, it is a common mistake for a speaker to make too much eye contact with any VIPs in an audience. Fight the temptation to look in their direction too regularly.

Speaking Position

What is the best position to adopt while presenting? My own view is that all speakers should present on their feet. Whenever a speaker stands up it increases the value and importance of what he or she has to say.

When you have finished and want to develop a question session or discussion, it is acceptable and extremely effective to change to a sitting position. Sitting down implies informality and makes question sessions and discussions more likely to develop. But always stand up to make your presentation.

There are a number of aspects relating to stance that are important.

Pacing

Some people develop, through nervous tension, a habit of pacing up and down the length of a platform. This can be a terrible distraction for the audience as their eyes follow the speaker from one side to another. It is a little like watching two tennis players in action, but with one performer the rocking motion can eventually cause the audience to drift into a relaxed state of sleepiness.

Another problem with this is that the pacer makes a great deal of eye contact, but with the floor, perhaps glancing in the direction of the audience from time to time just to make sure they are still there.

Obviously, movement is good, but as a guideline it should only be one pace from your central speaking point. Therefore, if you may be using a flip-chart, overhead projector or any other presentational aid, try always to position this one pace from your central speaking point.

Using a table or lectern

Some speakers like to make their presentations from behind a table, others prefer to work from a lectern. As far as a table is concerned, it does provide the speaker with a feeling of security but also creates a barrier between the speaker and the audience. Tables and lecterns have only one purpose, as a place on which to rest your notes, since it goes without saying that you should never be holding your notes. And while we are on that subject, you will no doubt have seen speakers who waggle their notes at the audience; or you may have attempted to count the pages of notes to see how long the speech is going to last. Don't let this happen in your presentation.

As a good guideline, always opt for a small lectern and try never to speak from behind a table. If there is no lectern available, select the smallest possible table and preferably speak from one side of it rather than from behind it.

If you have never used a lectern before, practise. Lecterns are not there to be leant on. If you do this you will appear to be preaching, which is acceptable in the pulpit but not in normal presentations. It is perfectly acceptable to be behind a lectern for the first few minutes and then gradually to move away from it as your speech progresses.

Posture

Distracting postures include:

▪ carrying all your weight on one leg;
▪ having one shoulder pointed to the audience, which makes you appear introverted;
▪ continually backing away.

The right posture is facing straight towards the audience.

Hand movements

Some speakers, particularly at the beginning of their speaking career, find that nervousness causes them to develop two uncontrollable objects at the end of their arms – their hands. Sometimes they are folded behind the speaker's back, sometimes they are folded in front, sometimes they go into trouser pockets and sometimes they play with coins or keys. It has been known for speakers to put a hand on their hip, or to pick their nose, pull an earlobe, or even scratch their backside!

Some people nervously fiddle with a ring and others hold on to a spring-loaded ballpoint pen that can make a distracting clicking sound, inaudible to the speaker but loud enough to drive an audience potty.

These are all major distractions that a speaker can be in control of.

Hands should be seen and always be in front of the body.

Good hand movements can complement and enhance the value of what is spoken. Speakers who synchronize their hand movements with their words will communicate more effectively.

Silence

One of the most powerful techniques that can be used in conversation as well as in public speaking is the use of silence.

If you have a very important point that you want to get across to your audience, pause for a second or two before stating your message and then, even more importantly, allow a few seconds of silence immediately afterwards. The silence before generates a feeling of expectation. The silence afterwards allows time for your message to be assimilated and thought about.

Sadly, many speakers devalue what may be an outstanding quotation or a strong message by not allowing sufficient pauses, silence or thinking time to let the audience take in the power of what has just been said.

If you are reading this book because you are about to attempt your first speech, you may think that all this sounds too difficult. Let me assure you that timing does come with practice, but don't worry too much about it. It is much more important to be enthusiastic and to be positive.

Enthusiasm

You will never lose if you combine sincerity with enthusiasm, as long as your enthusiasm is genuine, and you can maintain and build a positive attitude of mind by always looking for the good and expecting the best.

We live in a world where radio, TV and newspapers provide a daily dose of news of misery, strife, hunger and warfare from around the world. We can do very little about most of this suffering. There will always be people who say it's going to get worse. So, look for the good, concentrate on positive achievements, look to the future with hope and always convey to your audience a feeling of hope.

With the development of natural enthusiasm, you will become a great presenter. There are many outstanding speakers with little or no education, who are slightly inarticulate but have tremendous enthusiasm, and who are sought out by organizations throughout the world.

Pocket Reminders

- First gain the audience's acceptance
- Remember that a smile starts to remove the barriers
- Make sure the audience know how long your presentation will last
- Make your presentation seem like a public conversation rather than a public speech
- Maintain eye contact
- Make your presentation standing up
- Face the audience
- Synchronize your hand movements with your words
- Use silence
- Develop natural enthusiasm.

Wise Words

The greatest discovery of my generation is that human beings can alter their lives by altering their attitudes of mind.

William James

18

Develop Good Habits

By developing good habits, you can keep the audience on your side.

Use Personal Pronouns

The first good habit is careful use of the crucial words 'I', 'we', 'you' and 'they'.

The word 'I' should be used sparingly. It is best used when referring to your own past experience or mistakes. It is better not to use it in the context of building your own importance or how clever you may have been.

> The greatest speakers use 'I' very rarely.

Great speakers normally only use 'I' to help develop audience identification. What do I mean by audience identification? I mean finding and sharing some common ground with your audience. This common ground can be either experience or common interest, but it is extremely important in developing not only identification, but empathy.

The words 'we' and 'us' are 'good news' words and they communicate extremely well, so whenever you have good news to impart, use 'we', 'us', 'you' and 'your'. On the other hand, when you have bad news, when you are being critical or cynical or in any way negative, even if you are talking about a negative future tend, try always to use the word 'they'.

Keep to time

The second good habit is being totally professional in sticking to your allotted time. Many presentations have a printed programme with times for each session and your audience expect you to speak for the time given in the programme. Some conference organizers do not allow sufficient comfort breaks and members of the audience will wait until the end of a session before rushing to the loo. That's one very important reason to stick to your time.

Keep your speeches

The final good habit is to keep all your speeches. Always rewrite the text for each occasion, even though you may be speaking on exactly the same subject. The discipline of rewriting will help you to improve your presentation as well as refresh your memory and your subconscious mind.

By 'rewriting' I do not mean that you have to create a new presentation, but do remember that at every presentation the audience is slightly different and it is important that you appear to see things from each audience's point of view. You may be copying down exactly the same speech as you have given previously but, in the process, you will find you make one or two minor adjustments.

Pocket Reminders

▨ Use 'I' only sparingly
▨ 'We' and 'us' are good news words
▨ See things from the audience's point of view
▨ Keep to your allotted time
▨ Keep all your speeches.

Wise Words

The essence of skill is extracting meaning from everyday experience.

Author unknown

19

Ditch the Bad Habits

Let's look at some of the bad habits that not only will switch your audience off, but can also bore them into looking at their watches or even counting light bulbs in the ceiling.

Self-importance

One very effective method of losing audience identification is to build your own importance. For example, a speaker may say something like:

> Ladies and gentlemen, I now wish to talk to you about something on which I have been recognized as the world authority. I have had 20 years' experience and made numerous appearances on radio and TV, and books and articles have been written about my experiences.

Apologizing

You should not begin your speech with an apology. Everybody has heard the classic phrase 'Unaccustomed as I am...', but apologies come in many different forms.

■ 'I'm sorry I'm late.

▣ I'm sorry I'm unprepared.
▣ I have nothing very important to say.
▣ I'm sorry to take up your time.

Apologizing immediately devalues both the speaker and the presentation. If an apology in any form is due to an audience it is best done by the person introducing the speaker.

Giving Too Many Facts and Figures

When giving a presentation avoid relating streams of facts and figures. They will not be remembered, so the exercise is pointless. Of course many presentations depend on the speaker imparting facts and figures to support his or her message. If that is the case, the facts and figures must be presented in visual form, either on a slide, an overhead projector transparency, a flip-chart or in a handout.

Jargon

Avoid flowery words, in-company jargon or terminology that your audience may not be familiar with. At the same time you must be realistic. If terminology and abbreviations are expected and are the norm, then it is correct for the speaker to use them so as to communicate at the same level as his or her audience.

Jokes

Many people find that humour is important in a presentation, but let's be realistic – some people have the ability to tell a joke, or imitate an accent, or be a good raconteur, and others do not. If you are not confident of your joke-telling ability, avoid jokes.

The right joke in the right company in the right place can be extremely funny, but unless you are absolutely certain that a joke will be well received, don't tell it. Remember the phrase 'if in doubt, leave it out'.

Dirty jokes

Dirty jokes are definitely taboo.

Dirty jokes are one of the main causes of audience embarrassment and loss of acceptability for speakers. Don't tell them. (This is not simply a prudish comment.)

Snide comments

Making snide comments about a religion, a race or a political party is not so much a bad habit as a bad mistake and one that a speaker only makes once. If there is even one person in an audience who can be offended by a speaker's snide or unnecessary remarks, that speaker will lose empathy and audience identification. If you need to make critical comments as part of the presentation, use the third party.

Pocket Reminders

- Don't exaggerate your own importance
- Don't begin with an apology
- Don't smoke or drink alcohol before your presentation
- Don't bombard the audience with facts and figures
- Avoid irrelevant jargon
- Put yourself in your audience's shoes
- If in doubt, leave it out
- Don't offend your audience
- Keep the audience on your wavelength
- Use the third-party approach to criticism.

Wise Words

I hate fear so I eliminate the needless risks.

Jackie Stewart

Questions

Here we deal with handling questions from the audience and with taking questions from them. Let's first take the situation in which the speaker asks the audience a question.

Asking the Audience Questions

Many speakers find that they don't get the reaction they were hoping for because they don't lead the audience into responding. Take, for example, the question: 'Ladies and gentlemen, how many of you came here by car?' Does the speaker want people to put their hand up or respond verbally? If the desired reaction is that they should raise their hands, the speaker should raise his or her hand in the air first. The speaker must always lead from the front.

When the leaders are leading, the followers will follow.

Taking Questions

Now let's turn to the handling of questions from the audience. For many presenters, taking questions can be a harrowing experience. For others, it can become the most enjoyable part of their presentation. Therefore, to make question time a success, it is important that the speaker establishes the ground rules.

Let's suppose the speaker doesn't want questions during the presentation. The speaker or the person who makes the introduction should make this clear at the beginning of the presentation, saying, for example:

> Ladies and gentlemen, I anticipate there may be some points you wish to raise. We will therefore have time for questions at the end of my presentation, so please can you keep them until then.

If, on the other hand, the speaker doesn't want questions at all, how about this:

> Ladies and gentlemen, there may be some points you wish to raise at the conclusion of my presentation. I will be able to answer your questions personally on a one-to-one basis outside the scheduled proceedings, as I know some of you want to get away very quickly.

Techniques for handling questions

Always ask the audience whether they heard the question. A golden tip – regardless of whether the audience has heard the question, repeat it.

If you don't know the answer to a question, never try to make up an answer. Sometimes people who ask questions already know the answer. If you get it wrong, you lose enormous credibility, apart from confidence and control, and it can devalue an otherwise superb presentation. Here are two techniques to use when you don't know the answer to a question:

Say 'I am sorry, I don't know the answer to that question', and, depending on the importance of the question, you can say 'I will find out the answer for you' (and then make sure you do).

Alternatively, ask the audience to help. Say 'I am sorry, I don't know the answer to that question. Does anybody else know?'

> You will never lose respect from a person or an audience when you say 'I am sorry, I don't know the answer to that.'

Pocket Reminders

- Lead from the front
- Send difficult questions back
- Never make up an answer
- Prime someone to ask a question if necessary
- Never attack the questioner
- Keep smiling
- Never lose control.

Wise Words

An expert is a person who will know tomorrow why the things he predicted yesterday didn't happen today.

Author unknown

Richard Denny's books are all available from good booksellers or direct from the publishers at:

Kogan Page Ltd
120 Pentonville Road
London N1 9JN
Telephone: 020 7278 0433
Facsimile: 020 7837 6348
E-mail: kpinfo@kogan-page.co.uk
Website: www.kogan-page.co.uk

For further information on Richard Denny's books, videos, audiocassettes and CDs, please write to:

The Richard Denny Group
8 Cotswold Business Village
Moreton-in-Marsh
Gloucestershire
GL56 0JQ

Telephone: 00 + 44 (0)1608 812424
Facsimile: 00 + 44 (0)1608 651638
E-mail: success@denny.co.uk

Or visit the website www.denny.co.uk for your thought for the day.

Further Reading from Kogan Page

The Advanced Numeracy Test Workbook, Mike Bryon (2003)

Aptitude Personality and Motivation Tests: Assess Your Potential and Plan Your Career, 2nd edition, Jim Barrett (2004)

The Aptitude Test Workbook, Jim Barrett (2003)

The A-Z of Careers and Jobs, 12th edition, Susan Hodgson (2005)

Better Business Writing, Timothy V Foster (2002)

Career, Aptitude and Selection Tests: Match Your IQ, Personality and Abilities to Your Ideal Career, Jim Barrett (1998)

Dealing with Difficult People, Roy Lilley (2001)

Develop Your Assertiveness, 2nd edition, Sue Bishop (2000)

Develop Your NLP Skills, Andrew Bradbury (2000)

Developing Your Staff, Patrick Forsyth (2001)

The Effective Leader, Rupert Eales-White (2003)

Empowering People, 2nd edition, Jane Smith (2000)

The First-Time Manager: The First Steps to a Brilliant Career, 3rd edition, Michael Morris (2005)

The Graduate Psychometric Test Workbook, Mike Bryon (2005)

Great Answers to Tough Interview Questions, 6th edition, Martin Yate (2005)

How I Made It: 40 Successful Entrepreneurs Reveal All, Rachel Bridge (2004)

How People Tick: A Guide to Difficult People and How to Handle Them, Mike Leibling (2005)

How to be an Even Better Manager: A Complete A to Z of Proven Techniques & Essential Skills, Michael Armstrong (2004)

How to Manage Meetings, Alan Barker (2002)

How to Master Personality Questionnaires, 2nd edition, Mark Parkinson (2000)

How to Master Psychometric Tests, 3rd edition, Mark Parkinson (2004)

How to Motivate People, Patrick Forsyth (2000)

How to Pass Advanced Numeracy Tests, Mike Bryon (2002)

How to Pass Graduate Psychometric Tests, 2nd edition, Mike Bryon (2001)

How to Pass Numeracy Tests, 2nd edition, Harry Tolley & Ken Thomas (2000)

How to Pass Numerical Reasoning Tests: A Step-by Step Guide to Learning the Basic Skills, Heidi Smith (2003)

How to Pass Professional Level Psychometric Tests: Contains Practice Tests for IT, Management and Finance Recruitment, 2nd edition, Sam Al-Jajjoka (2004)

How to Pass Selection Tests, 3rd edition, Mike Bryon & Sanjay Modha (2005)

How to Pass Verbal Reasoning Tests, 2nd edition, Harry Tolley & Ken Thomas (2000)

How to Succeed at an Assessment Centre: Test-Taking Advice from the Experts, 2nd edition, Harry Tolley & Robert Wood (2005)

How to Write a Business Plan, Brian Finch (2001)

Improve Your Communication Skills, Alan Barker (2000)

IQ and Psychometric Test Workbook, Philip Carter (2005)

IQ and Psychometric Tests, Philip Carter (2004)

The Leader's Guide to Lateral Thinking Skills: Powerful Problem-solving Techniques to Ignite Your Team's Potential, Paul Sloane (2003)

Organise Yourself, John Caunt (2000)

Powerful Reports and Proposals, Patrick Forsyth (2003)

Preparing Your Own CV: How to Improve your Chances of Getting The Job You Want, 3rd edition, Rebecca Corfield (2003)

Readymade CVs: Sample CVs for Every Type of Job, 3rd edition, Lynn Williams (2004)

Readymade Job Search Letters: Every Type of Letter for Getting the Job you Want, 3rd edition, Lynn Williams (2004)

Shut Up & Listen!: The Truth about How to Communicate at Work, Theo Theobald and Cary Cooper (2004)

Successful Interview Skills: How to Present Yourself with Confidence, 4th edition, Rebecca Corfield (2006)

Successful Presentation Skills, 2nd edition, Andrew Bradbury (2000)

Successful Time Management, Patrick Forsyth (2003)

Team Building, Robert Maddux (2000)

The Ultimate Career Success Workbook: Tests and Exercises to Assess your Skills and Potential, Rob Yeung (2002)

The Ultimate CV Book: Write the Perfect CV and Get That Job, Martin Yate (2002)

The Ultimate Interview Book, Lynn Williams (2005)

The Ultimate Job Search Letters Book: Write a Perfect Letter and Get That Job, Martin Yate (2003)

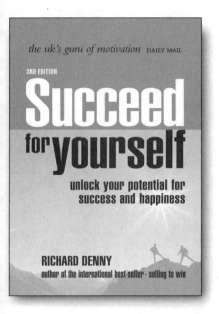

the uk's guru of motivation DAILY MAIL

3RD EDITION

Succeed
for yourself

unlock your potential for
success and happiness

RICHARD DENNY
author of the international best-seller - selling to win

"Each page is packed with easy to read common-sense advice on how to turn dreams into goals and goals into success."
—Roger Black

"Richard Denny is the master of motivation. If you read this book it will probably change your life."
—Rosemary Conley

0 7494 4436 3   Paperback   March 2006

Kogan Page is Europe's largest independent publisher of business books.

Kogan Page books cover every key business function – including management, marketing, branding, finance, sales, human resources, training, logistics, and transport – at every level from basic skills to high-level academic and professional texts. We also publish titles on careers and personal development, property, personal finance and general reference.

We have co-publishing relationships with many leading corporations, professional firms, media, institutions, professional bodies, and government and overseas agencies.

For further information on how to order, please visit
www.kogan-page.co.uk

KOGAN PAGE